HOW TO MAKE YOUR BOSS WORK FOR YOU

More than 200 Hard-Hitting Strategies, Tips, and Tactics to Keep Your Career on the Fast Track

Jim G. Germer

Business One Irwin
Homewood, Illinois 60430

This publication is designed to provide accurate and
authoritative information in regard to the subject matter
covered. It is sold with the understanding that neither the
author nor the publisher is engaged in rendering legal, accounting,
or other professional service. If legal advice or other expert
assistance is required, the services of a competent
professional person should be sought.

*From a Declaration of Principles jointly adopted by a Committee
of the American Bar Association and a Committee of Publishers.*

Senior editor: Jeffrey A. Krames
Project editor: Rebecca Dodson
Production manager: Diane Palmer
Designer: Tara L. Bazata
Compositor: Precision Typographers
Typeface: 11/14 Palatino
Printer: Arcata Graphics/Fairfield
All cartoons prepared by Robert J. Bauer.

Library of Congress Cataloging-in-Publication Data

Germer, Jim.
    How to make your boss work for you : More than 200 hard-hitting strategies,
tips, and tactics to keep your career on the fast track / Jim
Germer.
        p.   cm.
    Includes bibliographical references.
    ISBN 1-55623-417-1
    1. Career development. 2. Executive ability. 3. Organizational
behavior. 4. Office politics. I. Title.
HF5381.G486   1991
650.1—dc20   90–23917

Printed in the United States of America
1 2 3 4 5 6 7 8 9 0 AGF 8 7 6 5 4 3 2 1

Acknowledgments

Special thanks to:

THE U.S. JAYCEES

Jeffrey A. Krames, Kay Kipling, Fawn Germer Roth, Martha S. Fowler, and artist Robert J. Bauer

Eva Arfa, Scott Atkinson, Wayne Baer, Joanne Baltrip, Sam Bander, Charles Belvin, Donald Branum, Bill Brimmer, Jackie Broach, Danny Calhoun, Carl Chelstrom, Nancy Corrier, Charles W. Coxwell, Elizabeth T. Crawford, Lee Davis, Ed Dion, Becky Dodson, Deborah Dufresne, Joseph R. Dynlacht, Rhonda Edmonds, Todd S. Ellis, John Emmett, Jessee Estrada, Donald Branum, Connie Ferguson, David Foran, Gayle Fortin, Brian Gardner, Christina Garrison, Bill Gary, Michael Glass, Kevin D. Glass, Robin Gougler, Debbie Green, Herb Greenberg, Tom Hay, Bob Holiday, Steve Hopkins, Doug Hayes, Deidre S. Hettinger, Steve Ipsen, Wayne Janette, Robbie Johnston, Tom Kaper, Susan Kaplow, Peter Kurth, John Lopez, Gary Lucas, Rebecca Madeira, Mark Mandel, Chip Marra, Dan Markus, Scott Marsters, Steve Mathison, Bill Mays, Richard B. McKernan, Jim McMahon, Meredith

Nierenberg, Regula Noetzle, Juanita Pierottie, Charles Price, Katherine Ratti, Dr. Robert Reardon, Curt Riley, John Rogerts, Geoffrey Roth, Patty Rumpf, Bob Rusk, Steve Savage, Mary Ann Schwartz, Judith Sell, John Shiroma, Sissy Shull, Stuart J. Siegel, Jane Sigler, Paul Siska, Susan Springler, Steve Stevens, Rich Sussaman, Sandra Sweatt, Michael Taaffe, Dave Tyson, Thomas P. Van Auker, Tom Vaughn, Jane Webster, Joseph Wegeryznowski, Eva Weiss, and Hal Williams.

For my parents, Betty and Fred Germer,
and my sister, Fawn

Contents

Why This Book

It's a *different* corporate world out there. Thanks to a troubled economy and a glut of well-educated workers, career success has never been more elusive.

Millions of baby boomers are finding that today, it takes more than brains, talent, and hard work to get ahead. And they're not alone. Legions of new college graduates are finding that it takes a lot more than a college degree to make it in corporate America.

Teamwork, talent, and hard work are still prerequisites for career success. But today, a lot of other skills are just as important—skills such as career management, communications, attitude control, human relations, health enhancement, stress management, management development, and mastering office politics.

One problem, though. Those skills aren't taught in college. And the workplace doesn't usually teach them, either.

I wrote *How to Make Your Boss Work for You* to help you thrive in this different corporate world; a world in which you need individual advancement skills to get ahead. You can use those skills to complement important, traditional skills such as being a team player.

This book offers a comprehensive 10-part program for individual advancement. It addresses the career problems of employees and managers at all levels of the company ladder.

Remember, *everyone* is essentially an *employee*. You work for a boss who works—as an employee—for his or her boss. CEOs answer to stockholders. And the self-employed? Well, they answer to clients.

To get answers to your career problems, I surveyed nearly 1,000 men and women, interviewed more than 100 employees, and talked with more than 70 of the nation's leading experts on careers and the workplace. (See chapter 11 for survey results and methods.) Their stories gave birth to many of the principles and strategies found in this book. All of the participants had two things in common: they were open and honest, and they were not afraid to share their personal experiences and failures.

You might think this book is another "can do" book, full of inspiration and void of practical application, but it's not. It contains more than 200 practical, hard-hitting strategies, tips, and tactics for you to use throughout your career.

Here's what you'll learn:

- Strategies to master office politics.
- Shortcuts to break into middle or upper management.
- Specific ways to be more productive for your company.
- Tips to keep your career on the fast track.
- How to craft a winning personality, be more persuasive, and cope with difficult people.
- Ways to be a better public speaker and conversationalist.
- How to build health, energy, and stamina for a long, productive career.
- More important, you'll discover how to deal with success and how to cope with failure. . . . You may even become more self-confident.

Summaries, checklists, and examples make this book user-friendly and effective. If, however, you want to study a topic in greater detail, a reading list is provided at the end of the book.

Before you start reading Chapter 1, take a minute to reflect on your career. Think about what you've done right and what you've done wrong. Now think about where you want to go in life.

Let this book be a bridge between where you are now and where you want to go. May your journey across that bridge lead you to happiness and success.

Jim G. Germer
Bradenton, Florida

Chapter One

From Quicksand to Corner Office

N obody told you what kind of a jungle it really is out there. What happened to the fat paycheck and corner office you expected after your graduated?

You never thought it would be so hard, eh? Well, welcome to corporate America. It's time to climb out of the quicksand.

You belong to a generation of Americans that craves and expects success—lots of it. Unfortunately, not everyone is finding it.

Consider these facts and trends:

- Nearly 77 percent of U.S. workers earn less than $30,000 a year.*
- Most U.S. workers will probably have at least 7 to 10 jobs during their lifetimes.†

---

*U.S. Bureau of the Census Current Population Reports Series P-60#168, "Money Income and Poverty Status in the United States" (Bureau of the Census, 1989), p. 50.
†Robert Hall, "Importance of Lifetime Jobs in the U.S. Economy," *American Economic Review* (September 1982), pp. 716–724.

- Only 2 percent of all women and 10 percent of all men earn more than $50,000 a year. (How many live in high cost-of-living states like New York or California, or are in mature career stages?)*
- More than 50 percent of all new businesses fail within four years.**
- More than 85 percent of all real estate salespeople leave their original companies within three years.†
- Less than 15 percent of all professionals employed by "Big Six" CPA firms are partners.‡
- Between 40 and 50 percent of all new stockbrokers leave the brokerage business by the end of their third year.§
- About 29 percent of workers have spent less than one year working for their current employer. (Another 31 percent have spent only two to five years on the job.)#

Not surprisingly, more than one out of three people who responded to my career survey thought that their careers would have gone a lot farther since graduation day, and that they would now be collecting a much bigger paycheck.

There's a lesson to be learned here. And that lesson is that you *must* overcome the mental blocks standing between you and your career success. The wrong attitudes may cause you to hop from job to job, get fired, or even bomb out of the career game entirely.

Break out of career purgatory. Use this first chapter in your 10-part individual advancement program to help you:

Money Income and Poverty Status in the United States: 1989. Advance Data from the March 1990 Current Population Survey (Bureau of the Census, USGPO, 1990), p. 6.
**Small Business Administration (by Bruce Phillips), "Analysis of New Firms Survival and Growth," (May 1988), page 12.
†Herbert Greenberg, *What It Takes to Succeed in Sales: Selecting and Retaining Top Producers* (Homewood, IL: Dow Jones-Irwin, 1990), p.192.
‡"The Top 60 CPA Firms Survey," *Accounting Today,* September 1990, p. S6.
§National Association of Securities Dealers central registers depository database and Frank McAuliffe, December 18, 1990.
#U.S. Department of Labor News Release, "Most Occupational Changes Are Voluntary," October 22, 1987.

1. Control the New Breed attitudes that cause you to fail.
2. Make yourself more persistent, motivated, and confident.
3. Stop being a compulsive job changer and start succeeding at the job you already have.
4. Keep your self-confidence high after you fail.
5. Enjoy and build success.

PART ONE: NEVER STOP BELIEVING

WHY MANY BABY BOOMERS AND BUSTERS AREN'T MAKING IT

Chances are, your parents and grandparents place a premium on job security and company loyalty. They're part of the Old Breed. They lived through some pretty tough times: The stock market crash of 1929, the Depression, World War II.

After World War II ended, it was logical for the Old Breed to seek financial and emotional security. After years of doing without, the economy of the 1950s and 1960s geared itself to fulfill the needs of people who preferred to do *with*.

Companies expanded. They hired more employees, whom they viewed as assets to train. They offered stable employment in exchange for loyalty and hard work.

Duty-bound employees sought to advance up the corporate ladder, motivated by a drive for money and status. They expected promotions and raises as signs that they were appreciated.

Those were your parents' and grandparents' stories. Your story is much different. You're a New Breeder—you're not motivated by the need for security the way your parents were. Why not? Because you probably grew up with far more material assets than your parents.

How hard has life really been for you? Television, microwave ovens, and hundreds of other inventions may have offered you one of the most comfortable upbringings of any generation.

Characteristics of the Old Breed

- Motivated by security.
- Value changelessness.
- Lived through bad times such as World War II and the Depression.
- Loyal company people who worked for the same company for years.
- Worked for companies that valued them as employees.
- Crave money and status.
- Saved for the future.

Characteristics of the New Breed

- Motivated to pursue instant gratification.
- Not afraid to change.
- Grew up in a period of unprecedented prosperity.
- Never lived through many bad times.
- Usually work for a company only until a better opportunity comes along.
- Often quit activities prematurely because they're impatient for success.
- Fend for themselves.
- Big spenders who don't like to save for the future.

You're part of a New Breed that places a premium on self-fulfillment. A breed that believes, perhaps erroneously, that the future will be just as comfortable as the past. A breed that values change and is not willing to wait for success.

As a New Breeder, you have been programmed to fend for yourself. Mom and Dad may have stuck with one company until retirement—but not you. You work for a company only until the next opportunity comes along.

You've seen firsthand how companies abandon their employees. Legions of loyal company men and women have been put to pasture during economic downturns, mergers, and reorganizations.

Sure, you're a New Breeder; you operate under a new set of rules. But those rules can spell "doom" if you're not careful. They may have programmed you to self-destruct in your career drive.

HOW NEW BREED UPBRINGINGS CAUSE FAILURE

OK, enough of this definition stuff. Let's look at some ways New Breed upbringings sabotage careers.

Lack Motivation and Loyalty.   I am most important. I don't really care what happens to the company.

Well . . . yes and no. Yes, because companies *don't* stand by their employees the way they used to. No, because you cut your own throat if you hop from job to job.

Take Annette, for example:

I went to work for a major accounting firm after college. The recruiter was right; I got great experience. But the pay was lousy, and the hours were long. Then a client enticed me to take a job that paid nearly $6,000 more a year. Not bad, considering I'd have to work less hours.

Later, a headhunter coaxed me to accept another job, as an assistant controller at another company. I hated the job. My co-workers didn't like me and I had to work a lot of overtime. I decided to cut my losses so I started looking for another job.

Surprise! This time around, companies were afraid to hire me.

You see, I was no longer perceived as a fresh-faced kid just out of college. Instead, employers saw me as a woman who has had three jobs in five years. They think I'll leave them as soon as a better job comes along.

In order to move up the ladder, you must demonstrate real commitment. Shortcuts can be costly. So costly that you might not make it to the next level.

Feel Compelled to Tackle Problems Alone.   Can't take constructive criticism? Feel you have to do everything yourself? Afraid to
get help?

Self-oriented people are often reluctant to ask people for help.
This can be devastating because they may be dooming themselves
to fail. How ironic. They might have succeeded had they just asked
for help.

Take Roger, for example. He was struggling with his first entry-
level job and wasn't getting his work done on time. With scant job
knowledge, he was afraid to ask questions. He worried that if he
did, people would notice that he couldn't do his job.

So he faked competence—for a while. Then it was too late—his
supervisor noticed his sloppy work.

Since Roger hadn't tried to improve job performance by seeking
help, his supervisor saw no reason to keep him. Why should he
keep Roger on the payroll? He didn't even care about his job
enough to seek help to do it properly.

Demand Instant Success and Excitement.   Quit. Quit. Quit. . . .
Baby boomers are gaining a reputation as a generation of quitters.
Why? They expect fast results in exchange for very little effort.

Too many people change jobs are careers in the same way an in-
vestor speculates with stocks and bonds: I'll be a programmer. . . .
That's the field for me. I'll be in real estate. . . . I'll get a job in public relations. . . . I'll be an engineer. "Whatever the fad is, these
people are looking for a quick fix," says Diana Richman, a clinical
psychologist with the Institute of Rational Emotive Therapy in
New York City.[1]

Here's one example.

Linda thought she would have made it into upper management by
now. A single mother with a child to support, she'd changed jobs a lot.

A few years ago, she went back to school to get her MBA. Night
school, however, was a big inconvenience. She quit.

Then she got her securities license. "I thought this was my big
chance," says Linda. "At last, I could set my own hours. And dreams
of big commission checks filled my head.

"I worked hard, But in spite of making thousands of cold calls, I opened very few accounts. With no big commission checks in sight, I quit the brokerage business. I couldn't handle the rejection.

"I then took a job as marketing director for a retirement complex. I thought it was going to be a great opportunity. But I couldn't make my quota. So I left that job, too."

Now Linda works in the sales department of a major hotel. "Good benefits, but I still earn less than 30 grand a year."

Sound familiar? Ward off New Breed desires for immediate success. Don't foolishly indulge them; you may end up in career purgatory like Linda.

Procrastinate. Some people try to escape from monotonous or unpleasant duties by procrastinating. They often pass off unpleasant duties onto someone else. And they put off making decisions or performing important activities because they fear making mistakes.

Regardless if why they do it—it's still a no-class way to fail.

When you procrastinate, you only create more problems for yourself. You'll be anxious and frustrated if you feel pressed to complete a project on time. Worse yet, your fear of work might cause you to do a sloppy job. And you know what that leads to!

Fear of Failure. Many New Breeders bomb out of activities and never rebound. They condemn themselves to low-level jobs because they fear failing again.

After nine years with the company, Bob, a sales trainer, was fired. Bob was devastated. So devastated that he didn't want to put himself in a position in which he might fail again.

Instead of another corporate job that might have taken better advantage of his skills and abilities, Bob wanted a safe job he was sure he could do. He got a job teaching drivers' education in a suburban Detroit high school.

Now, I *don't* mean to imply that teaching drivers' education isn't a noble profession. It's just that compared with Bob's previous skills and abilities, teaching drivers' education makes for a dramatic and perhaps unnecessary career change.

For some people, such a career change can be healthy. But for others, it may be a cop-out, an attempt to protect themselves from the pain of future failures by settling for safe jobs.

False Sense of Independence.   No one likes being told what to do. You probably didn't like it as a child, and you probably don't like it as an adult, either.

You're self-motivated. But you must accept the implicit power that your boss has over your career.

You make a big mistake if you sabotage yourself with ''Who is he to tell me what to do?'' New Breed attitudes. Those attitudes can be cataclysmic with a boss who is accustomed to Old Breed employees.

Fear of Failure

Fear of failure is cancerous to success. Don't be a victim. Here's a quiz to stop it before it stops you.

Are You Holding Yourself Back?

- Do you make remarks like, ''Money and success aren't important''?
- Do you pass up opportunities because you're afraid you won't be any good at them?
- Do you think it's wrong to make a mistake?
- Do you blame other people or events for your lack of success?
- Do you choose to stick with activities you are sure you can do?
- Do you put off doing activities?
- Do you stay with an unchallenging job or position?
- Do you fail to implement your major goals in life?
- Does your self-esteem depend entirely on your career success or failure?

Knock out fear of failure before it destroys you. If you can't manage it on your own, get professional help.

FLOUNDERING? HERE'S HOW TO MAKE YOURSELF MORE PERSISTENT

OK now you know how a New Breed upbringing may be causing you to underachieve. You don't have to spend your life in career purgatory. You can succeed. You can get back on the fast track. But you must control the New Breed desires of instant gratification.

The magic word for success is, of course, *persistence*. Here's how to reprogram yourself for success.

TIP
How to Make Yourself More Persistent

- Ward off New Breed impulses that tell you to quit too soon.
- Stop speculating in the job market; realize no job will be perfect.
- Set realistic goals for yourself.
- Have a definite vision of where you want to go.
- Don't let criticism and rejection destroy you.
- Adopt a healthy lifestyle. (If you feel good, you can put up with more dirt.)
- Pick a career that is fun for you, not one that is just a good way to make money.
- Choose a career where your personality clicks with the organization.
- Work for a company that appreciates you.
- Score part of the action. Find a company that lets you participate in decisions that affect your career.
- Stay away from boring jobs with few advancement opportunities.
- Persistence is a numbers game. (For example, if you're looking for a new job, send out 100 resumes, not 10 resumes.)
- Get counseling at an employee assistance program.

USE PERSISTENCE TO SOLVE YOUR CAREER PROBLEMS

In the long run, you have more to gain when you're willing to work hard for something. You *must* force yourself to endure periods of nonsuccess.

Refuse to quit a new job prematurely. You may blow an opportunity if you give in to New Breed impulses by quitting a job because of your impatience.

Most work situations aren't totally hopeless. So here's a plan to salvage jobs you're tempted to quit:

Cope with Criticism.   Don't get upset by criticism—if it's warranted. When someone tells you to improve your performance, always ask yourself: What am I doing that is creating this negative feedback?

The first real step toward solving career problems is to assess what your contribution is to those problems. In some ways, you may actually perpetuate them.

Change Work Habits.   Face it. You can't blame your work habits on office politics.

Work at improving the quality of your work effort: Get projects done on time. Make a conscious effort to get organized. Ask more questions. Avoid long lunches, coming in late, and leaving early. . . . and your total work performance can improve.

Change Attitudes.   The clergy and therapists may be sympathetic about depression and lack of productivity, but most bosses are not. Your private life may be in complete chaos, and you may hate your job, but employers still demand a day's work for a day's pay.

You may have to change your attitude if it negatively affects your job performance. Maintaining a positive attitude is hard work, but it can be done. Consider the alternative.

Improve Relations with Co-workers.   Even abrasive people can make themselves more congenial. Sometimes this can be done simply by saying, ''good morning,'' or smiling more often.

From Quicksand to Corner Office   **11**

Here are a few suggestions to point you in the right direction:

- Rub people the wrong way? Take a good course in human relations; read Chapter 3 of this book.
- Have problems getting ideas across? Take additional speech courses or try Toastmasters; read Chapter 4.
- Need help dealing with bosses and co-workers? Consider taking an assertiveness training course.

Change Expectations. ''Where is the evidence that you should have a boss that you like or that all your co-workers *should* be to your liking?'' asks Diana Richman.[2]

There is a big difference between accepting and liking people and events at work. You may have to work with someone who is

---

STRATEGY
The Myth of the Perfect Job

You probably loathe some aspects of your career and job. Who doesn't? No job is perfect. But you must learn to live with some negatives in the workplace.

Recognize that conditions will never be exactly right. Some jobs have great working conditions but skimpy salaries and benefits. Other jobs work fingers to the bone but pay well.

Use the *Esquire* test (see the next section) to help you rate your job from 1 to 10. (The lowest possible score is 0; the highest possible score is 10.56.) If your score is six or higher, consider yourself lucky—you're probably ahead of the game.

Job changing in search of a score higher than six is often futile. Thousands of people have had less than brilliant careers because they hopped from job to job in search of the perfect one. In fact, you may be better off trying to succeed in the job you now have rather than being a career gypsy.

Remember, most people never find the perfect job. So don't speculate in the job market. You might be pursuing a nirvana that does not exist.

**The Great Esquire
Job Happiness
Quotient Test**

You must answer every question!

PART A: SENSE OF ACCOMPLISHMENT

That's That's
me   not me

That's me	That's not me	
☐	☐	Most days, I look forward to going to work in the morning.
☐	☐	I feel that I use my best talents in my job.
☐	☐	My job gives me the freedom to pursue a good idea.
☐	☐	My job gives me the mental challenge I need.
☐	☐	Little of the work I do is tedious.
☐	☐	My job gives me the opportunity to grow professionally.
☐	☐	My job gives me the opportunity to teach the ropes to others.
☐	☐	My job gives me the level of excitement and adventure I require.
☐	☐	I am proud of the work I do.
☐	☐	My job gives me the opportunity to make decisions.
☐	☐	Within the last two years, I have received a promotion, a major pay raise, or other significant perks.
☐	☐	Without me, the company would suffer.
☐	☐	If I were paid less and had a less important title, I would still enjoy my work.
☐	☐	I feel that the work I do contributes to the good of society.
☐	☐	If my company moved to another city, I would want to move with it.

Please add up the number of answers in the left-hand column.
Sense of accomplishment = A = ___

PART B: AMBITION

Please enter the number that correctly reflects the extent to which the following statements apply to you:

1	2	3	4	5
THAT'S NOT ME				THAT'S ME

___ Someday soon, I'd like to have my boss's job. (If you are the boss, enter 5.)
___ When people in comparable positions with mine succeed, I tend to be jealous and angry.
___ I want to make a lasting mark on my field.
___ I want to be famous.
___ I want to be rich.
___ I don't like taking vacations.
___ I believe hard work gets you further than luck.
___ I could do my boss's job better than he/she can. (If you are the boss, enter 5.)
___ I want to be considered one of the best in my field.
___ I am a workaholic.

__ I often worry that I am an underachiever.
__ Career success is more important to me than enjoying my life.
__ I can't really enjoy my personal life if work is not going well.
__ I want to be powerful.
__ My job is my greatest source of pleasure.
__ If things aren't right at home, I can always find solace if things are going well at work.
__ If things are going badly at work, my homelife is always affected.
__ I'm in this company for the long haul. (If you work for yourself, enter 5.)
__ I believe whatever sacrifices I make now will be rewarded later.
__ I have no trouble playing hardball when I have to.
__ I am achieving what I want to achieve.

Please add up your answers.
Ambition = B = __

PART C: STRESS

Please fill in the number that reflects how often you have the following experiences:

1	2	3	4	5	6	7
NEVER	ONCE	RARELY	SOMETIMES	OFTEN	USUALLY	ALWAYS

_ Being tired.
_ Feeling depressed.
_ Having a bad day.
_ Being totally bored.
_ Not having the time to have fun.
_ Being short tempered.
_ Feeling trapped.

_ Feeling angry.
_ Feeling rejected.
_ Feeling lethargic.
_ Feeling anxious.
_ Being under constant and unrealistic time pressures.
_ Feeling overqualified for my job.
_ Feeling inadequate.

Please add up your answers.
Stress = C = __

PART D: YOUR WORK ENVIRONMENT

The following questions measure what you think of your work environment. For this section, answer only the set of questions that pertains to your job status:

1	2	3	4	5
FALSE				TRUE

If you work for someone else:

__ I have not been hindered because of my race, sex, or sexual preference.
__ I like my colleagues.
__ I respect my boss.
__ My boss always looks me in the eye when he/she is talking to me.
__ My company always rewards good work.
__ I see a strong opportunity for promotion in the near future.
__ My company is successful.
__ I am satisfied with the company's health-insurance plan.

__ My office is a pleasant environment in which to work.
__ My company puts out an excellent product.

If you work alone:

__ I rarely miss the interaction of colleagues.
__ My work environment makes it easy for me to concentrate.
__ I am able to maintain a division between my work life and my personal life.
__ I don't need competition to spur me on.
__ I hate being told what to do.
__ I am proud when I tell a new acquaintance what I do.
__ I know what others expect of me, and I meet their expectations.
__ I've never missed being a team member.
__ I do damned good work and realize that few people know I exist. I like it that way.
__ I enjoy working alone.
__ I don't have the stomach for office politics.

If you are the boss:

__ I can trust my employees with major responsibilities.
__ Conversation rarely comes to a halt when I walk into a room.
__ I feel that my leadership is appreciated by my employees.
__ I am satisfied with my company's performance.
__ I think being consistent with my employees is important.
__ My employees recognize that my criticism is directed toward the job they do and is not the result of a personality clash.
__ Let's be honest: It's a hell of a lot easier to command by inspiring enthusiasm than by inspiring fear.
__ I have clearly defined goals for my company, and I feel my employees understand what they are.
__ I think a good boss should also be a teacher.
__ Though it's busy here, I have no problem taking a vacation.

Please add up your answers.
Work environment = D = __

PART E: ARE YOU WORKING TOO MANY HOURS?

1	2	3	4	5
FEWER THAN 35	35–44	45–54	55–64	65 OR MORE

__ How many hours do you work a week?
(Please enter the number corresponding to your hours bracket.)

Please enter the appropriate number:

1	2	3	4	5
THAT'S NOT ME				THAT'S ME

__ I work too many hours.   __ I work into the night.
__ I work on weekends.   __ I work on vacations.

Please add up all five numbers.
Hours worked = E = __

That's the end of the test. Now we'll take your answers and calculate your Job Happiness Quotient. To arrive at a final number, we'll need some vital statistics.

Your age: 21–32 = **1**   33–43 = **2**   44–54 = **3**   55+ = **4**

Please enter the number corresponding to your age bracket.
Age = F = __

Your Salary:

under $20,000 = 1	$60,000–$69,999 = 6
$20,000–$29,999 = 2	$70,000–$79,999 = 7
$30,000–$39,999 = 3	$80,000–$89,999 = 8
$40,000–$49,999 = 4	$90,000–$99,999 = 9
$50,000–$59,999 = 5	$100,000 or more = 10

Please enter the number corresponding to your salary bracket.
Salary = G = __

Now fill in the values:

Accomplishment	= **A** = __	Hours	= **E** = __
Ambition	= **B** = __	Age	= **F** = __
Stress	= **C** = __	Salary	= **G** = __
Work Environment	= **D** = __		

And enter those values in the following equation:

$$3.6 + \frac{A + G}{F \times 6} + \frac{B - C}{70} + \frac{(D/5) - 5}{3} - \frac{E}{30} = JHQ$$

In other words:

$$3.6 + \frac{\text{Accomplishment} + \text{Salary}}{\text{Age} \times 6} +$$

$$\frac{\text{Ambition} - \text{Stress}}{70} + \frac{(\text{Work environment}/5) - 5}{3} -$$

$$\frac{\text{Hours}}{30} = \text{Job happiness quotient}$$

Lowest possible score: **0**   *Highest possible score:* **10.56**

What it means:
10 You're in heaven. Stay there.
 9 You're in heaven, with the rare glitch. When it comes up, deal with it.
 8 You're knocking on heaven's gate.

7 Get real! Whatever minor gripes you have, you're a lot happier than most of your colleagues.
6 Sure, you've got some problems, but don't complain. You've got it pretty good, all things considered. Decide what you can do to make your current situation better.
5 So it's neither as bad nor as good as you thought. Try asking people in other departments about their work. It could be that you don't need to change your job, but your assignment.
4 You're teetering on the cusp of misery. Explore your options. Don't turn down a better offer.
3 Hit the phones. Start networking. Call your local headhunter.
2 Do the words *working stiff* mean anything to you?
1 What are you waiting for? It's time to move on.

Source: First appeared in *Esquire*, April 1990. Reprinted courtesy of the Hearst Corporation.

---

nosy. You may have a boss who takes credit for your ideas. Perhaps you have to work a lot of overtime you don't get paid for. These things aren't under your control, but you can learn to live with them.

How? First, focus on what you *can* change about your plight. For example, if you share an office with an abrasive co-worker, request to share an office with a more congenial person. Try to be more productive during each day. Work at attracting more attention to your ideas.

Second, if the changes you've made don't improve your problem, you may have to lower your expectations. "The world isn't perfect. Sometimes you have to live with frustration," says Dr. Bernard Weiner, a professor of psychology at UCLA.[3]

WHEN IS IT TIME TO QUIT?

Some motivational speakers tell people, "Don't listen to your critics," or "Don't think of failure when you pursue a goal," or "You're only a failure if you quit." Good advice, but it doesn't apply to all people and all situations.

While I've stressed that failure isn't all bad, you need to bail out of some activities while you still have time. Once you carry a failure to the point of cataclysm, it's too late to reduce the impact of that failure.

People reap disastrous results when they hold on to an unmanageable business too long. They delude themselves into believing that they will be able to turn things around with simple fine-tuning. Meanwhile, they can't pay their bills, incur the wrath of their creditors, and end up losing their homes or businesses.

A positive attitude doesn't mean lying to yourself. Don't deny negative feedback when it indicates that you probably won't achieve a major career goal.

When is it time to quit? W. C. Fields, the late comedian, said it best, "If at first you don't succeed, try, try again. Then quit. There's not use being a damn fool about it."

Before you throw in the towel, here are a few things to consider:

- Get as much information as you can. Be realistic. Try to make the best possible assessment of the situation.
- Compare your situation to what is happening to people who share your dilemma. And make sure you compare yourself with the right people. If you're just starting a new career, compare yourself with other rookies, not old pros.
- Look at the pattern of your own behavior over time. Ask yourself: Are you speculating in the job market? Are you interpreting failure incorrectly? If yes, you may want to stick it out longer.
- Make sure you have realistic expectations. It's frustrating to go from failure to failure. "You can hang in a job or occupation and finally succeed or you can hang in too long and be a failure all your life," says Dr. Weiner.[4]
- Realize that there's nothing wrong with quitting. Make sure you quit for a good reason and that quitting isn't the story of your life.

CASH IN ON FAILURE

Elbert Hubbard once said "A failure is a man who has blundered but is not able to cash in on the experience.* Many people have

---

*The New Lexicon Webster's Dictionary of the English language (New York: Lexicon Publications, Inc., 1988), p. QD-40.

never had to deal with a major league failure. When it happens, they're not prepared. For them, failing is brutal, and sometimes they never recover from it.

Here are some tips to deal with failure. Use them to get back on your feet quicker.

Don't Put Yourself Down.   You may be worrying what people will think of you. You may also worry about what's going to happen next. Even if you feel that your boss was a total jerk, it is normal to blame yourself for more than your fair share. Don't.

Be Objective and Compassionate.   Don't dwell on thoughts like What is wrong with me? I didn't try hard enough, I'm not a good manager, or I used the wrong strategy, Instead, ask yourself these questions: Did I do the best that I could at the time? Did I make mistakes? If I made mistakes, what can I learn from them?

Emphasize what went wrong in the process leading to why you failed. Don't mourn your messes.

Instead, try to examine why something didn't work and think how you can avoid making the same mistakes next time. Ask yourself What can I get that is positive from this experience? How is the knowledge I got out of this experience going to help me the next time?

Make Failure Your Friend.   Failure has a lot of value because it's a strong teacher. When you learn a lesson the hard way, you're not likely to forget it. Figure out what you can do the next time to prevent a similar failure from occurring.

Try Harder Next Time.   Challenge yourself to a level of performance that you can achieve. When you do this, you'll probably be more satisfied with your performance. In some ways, you may be able to reexamine a failure and find that you were more successful at that task than you thought you were.

Don't Rationalize.   Try not to blame events on other people. People who do this may believe that some person or event sabotaged their chances for success. They like to think that if they were given another chance, surely they would get it right. These people often come out fighting with their fists clenched and say things like, "How dare he tell me that! I'll show him. I'll just quit, and get a job at some other company that know how to treat its employees better. I don't need this hassle."

Blaming people and circumstances, even if they were to blame, usually doesn't help your cause. All those negative feelings steal time and energy that could be spent on other tasks.

Stop Feeling Sorry For Yourself. You'll have some negative emotions, of course. But if you see that you are not doing anything about taking care of yourself, take a look at your emotions and behavior. Are they productive? Or are you just dwelling on how it should have been and not doing anything about it?

If the answer to the last question is yes, you may be wasting valuable energy blaming external reasons instead of taking charge of your own career. You might need to talk with an understanding friend or seek professional help.

NEVER STOP BELIEVING IN YOURSELF

After you bomb, it may feel like it is the end of Western civilization. But force yourself to keep your self-confidence high.

Remind yourself that there are plenty of tasks that you can do well. Pretend you're a defense attorney and build a defense for your major client—you. Put yourself on the witness stand. And make sure you get a fair trial.

Now as the attorney, ask yourself: Are you a totally incompetent person? What are some things you've been successful at? Do you have a nice family? Do you have a nice car, house, boat, whatever?

By now you can see what my message is. You never want to stop believing in yourself. After a career setback, motivate yourself to look at positive things that suggest that you're a successful person instead of a loser or a rotten human being.

Maybe a career wasn't right for you or your ability didn't mesh with some task. But you have to believe that failure is only one part of your life. Other factors make up your self-esteem and self-confidence.

Sure, you still will feel down for a while. But your self-esteem that you've fought to keep high, despite challenges to the contrary, will help you to bounce back sooner.

PART TWO: DEALING WITH SUCCESS

In the American scheme of things, you have to be *number one.* No one cares about who went bankrupt last week. There's always another billionaire of the moment on the cover of *Fortune.* And they don't put the bronze medalist on cereal boxes.

Americans often believe that successful people must continue to improve their skills and abilities. Nowhere is this more prevalent than in the business world, where you're only as good as your last assignment, quota, or performance review.

You are under constant pressure to keep pushing yourself to higher levels. Management often puts everything that is in the past—well—in the past.

Companies expect you to be smarter and to do your job better now than you did last year. And since they often keep raising the standard of "acceptable" performance, a level that was acceptable last year may be considered mediocre this year.

This attitude—what have you done for me lately?—forces people to fail, to fear failure, and not to enjoy success. Why? Because if you don't keep improving your skills and performance, you might be put out to pasture.

Don't be lulled into a false sense of security if you're an average employee. Sooner or later, the company will likely replace you with someone better. Throughout your career monitor what your boss expects from you for the next year. If the expectations appear unattainable, speak up. You may be able to get some objectives re-evaluated. And keep reminding yourself that despite the pressure put on you to be number one, you're OK.

The Report Card of Success

Grade	Amount of Raise	What It Really Means
A	Merit raise	Candidate for promotion
B	Cost of living raise	Try harder next year
C	Paltry raise	Change or you won't be here two years from now
D	No raise	Start packing your bags

PROBLEMS WITH SUCCESS

Here are some more problems people have dealing with success:

Viewing Success as a Failure. Suppose you "plateau"—your abilities reach a level in which they don't get any better. You might fear that the people who pay your salary will think, "We gave him a raise, but he is doing less work," or "Well, she has a lot of ability, but she never seems to get any better."

This is a big problem for professional athletes. They are constantly being compared with other athletes who have become superstars. When someone gets blown away by a superachiever, people say that he hasn't lived up to his potential.

If people don't meet these high expectations, they're considered failures. How ironic. Each one did a good job, but a good job isn't good enough.

"When you start out doing well, you can only get so much better," says Dr. Edward R. Hirt, a psychology professor at the University of Wisconsin. "You might consider a successful effort of yours to be a failure because other people didn't acknowledge that it was that much of a success."[5]

Don't allow your self-image to be held hostage by other people's aberrant definition of success. Avoid concentrating on beating the other guy, and comparing yourself unfairly with other people.

Instead, set goals that are just for you, and gradually increase your goals over time.

Not Understanding Success.   If you don't have a good sense of why you succeeded at some task, you often assume that you are practically guaranteed to be just as successful the next time.

Not true. Even though you often don't know why you were successful in the past, you are still under pressure to maintain that success in the future.

You may be underconfident the next time you try that activity. After all, perhaps this will be the time people find out that you don't know anything.

After you complete a successful effort, spend some time evaluating exactly why you were successful. This can help you build the self confidence you need to repeat the success later.

Some Call It the Impostor Theory.   People with low self-esteem have problems dealing with success. In spite of their success, they often believe that they are charlatans or impostors.

They may feel that their success was an accident and that they're not worthy of success. They worry that all the good things that have been happening will disintegrate once people find out what frauds they really are.

If this sounds familiar, get professional help. You need to build more self-esteem for yourself before you self-destruct your career—or worse.

Dealing with People Who Envy Your Success.   Sometimes you have to play down your success. Learn from celebrities who must maintain friendships with non-celebrity friends and family. The smart ones learn to put a muzzle on their egos. This often means taking a back seat to people you might intimidate if you indulge yourself in ego gratification.

"My husband couldn't deal with the fact that I was earning a lot more money than he was," says Rebecca, a financial consultant. "I felt that he would rather have me miss promotions—just to maintain the status quo. That marriage ended."

"I still earn more than my second husband, but I don't rub it in his face. I try to stress that I love him for what he is. It helps to emphasize that the more money I make, the more money we make. This means nicer cars and more vacations together."

HOW TO KEEP WINNING, ACHIEVING, AND SUCCEEDING

Surprisingly, many people have problems dealing with success. Seems strange, but everything boils down to selfesteem. You must fight to get it. And you must fight to keep it high.

Here are some tips on how to enjoy success more:

Enjoy Success More

- Analyze why you were successful at a task. This helps you to repeat the success later.
- Accept that some people will be envious.
- Don't brag. Babbling on and on about your success turns people off.
- Don't be so goal oriented that you don't enjoy the goals you achieve. Buy something nice for yourself when you reach a goal, or get a promotion or a raise.
- Find someone to share your success with.
- Stay healthy. You're nothing without health.
- Fight to keep your self-esteem high. Get counseling if you can't do this on your own.
- Don't give in to self-destructive impulses. Celebrate what's right in your life, rather than mourn what's wrong.

AT A GLANCE

You don't have to be a washout in the success and failure department. Here's how to get out of career purgatory.

1. Ward off New Breed impulses that tell you to sabotage your career.
2. Make yourself more persistent, motivated, and confident.
3. Stop being a compulsive job changer and start succeeding at the job you already have.
4. Keep your self-confidence high after you bomb out of an activity.
5. Work at enjoying and building success.

CHAPTER 1   Author Interviews

1. Diana Richman, September 13, 1988.
2. Ibid.
3. Bernard Weiner, September 19, 1988.
4. Ibid.
5. Edward R. Hirt, September 22, 1988.

Chapter Two

Mastering Office Politics

D uring the 1950s and 1960s, often all it took to get a job and climb the ladder was basic competence. There was no fast track. Today, a college degree gets you a job interview. Strategy, as well as talent, are the tools that can get you ahead.

Simply working hard and knowing a lot is no guarantee of a place at the top. There is no shortage of talented baby boomers and baby busters in corporate America.

Everybody is educated. Everybody has talent. Everybody dresses for success. Want a job at the top? Get in line.

You are a New Breeder and you are trapped in ''corporate gridlock.''

The challenge is to break from the pack and still be a team player. And that means mastering office politics.

Office politics is an art. The masters know how to protect their turf, get along with difficult people, and expand their sphere of influence without making enemies. Ruthless people who misuse the principles of office politics may make quick leaps up the ladder. But along the way, they often trip over themselves, going just a little bit too far to get what they want.

It is no secret that some self-serving people choose to spread untrue rumors, withhold information, or play up to the boss at some-one's expense. You don't have to do it their way.

On the other hand, some workers ignore office politics, thinking that if they do a good job, others will notice and reward them. How naive.

It takes strategy to succeed. Use this second chapter in your individual advancement program to manage difficult people, reap the credit you deserve, and be a climber. Here are some strategies that will help you break from the pack:

HOW TO GET NOTICED

Think of all the long hours and hard work you gave your company. and for what? Has anybody noticed? Not unless you have told them to recognize you. *"Look At Me!"* you must say. Promote yourself, because nobody else will.

Most of all, you must impress the people who have the power to advance your career. You should also expand your influence outside the company with potential employers, clients, and community leaders. Your exposure outside the company in professional organizations and civic groups can help you find clients for your firm, valuable connections and, should you need them, job offers.

"You always have to be cognizant of opportunities," says Ronald C. Pilenzo, president of the Society for Human Resource Management. "What you really have to do is to think strategically about opportunities where you can let your superiors know who you are, what you are, and how good you are at it."[1]

Some people are too humble to take the credit they deserve. They fear others may consider them to be immodest or braggarts. There is some truth in their fear. As a result, handle your public relations in a subtle way. Blow your own horn, but don't blow it so loud that you nauseate the people you're trying to impress.

Here are some ways to get noticed:

Keep Your Boss Informed.   Send memos to your boss about projects you work on. A short note to your boss that summarizes your progress—for example, ''I thought you'd like to know that I finished the XYZ account ahead of schedule''—can get you some great PR. It is usually better to write a memo than to just tell your boss about the results of a project. A written memo is likely to end up in your personnel file. This will help your boss to remember all your accomplishments when it is time for your performance evaluation.

While it is always a good idea for you to keep your boss informed of your progress, it is an even better idea to have an independent third party do it for you. Secretaries, colleagues, and clients can give your boss valuable information about your accomplishments.

Build a Network of Supporters. Join many different business, charitable, and civic organizations for the service you can provide

to others. Community service gives you a good feeling, and it's good for business because you meet hundreds of people who learn your name and what you do for a living. Your service builds a dynamic network of goodwill ambassadors who promote you and your company.

Volunteer.   Managers both inside and outside your department are always on the lookout for competent people. Here are a few ways to attract their attention.

- Volunteer to work on special projects.
- Join a company task force.
- Attend optional meetings.
- Write original business plans and proposals (even if you have to write them on your own time).

Make the Media Your Ally.   You've seen those columns in the newspaper: "Achievers," "Business Briefs," and "Doers." Do you think the newspaper sent a reporter around town to ask every company who they promoted? No! Those columns are compilations of press releases sent by self-promoters. The really smart self-promoters also send a black-and-white glossy photograph to go along with the story.

Send press releases when you attend a special seminar, complete a specialized course, change jobs, or win an award. You will be surprised how often an achievement ends up in the newspaper.

TIP

Don't Alienate Bosses and Co-Workers

When it comes to getting noticed at work, use common sense. Strategies that make you a superstar in one company might get you the boot from another. There is no substitute for good judgment.

TACTIC

Corporate Climbers Are Team Players

I asked five leading management authorities, ''Can someone use an individual advancement program and still be a team player?''
Here's how they answered:
Thomas R. Horton, chairman and CEO of the American Management Association, answered:

> I think they are very compatible. In the United States, there are so-called unsupervised work teams or superteams where you not only have to be a team player, but you have to give a real individual contribution.
> The best team player is very likely to be the one that is going to be promoted in the future. Part of individual growth training is how to be a team player.[2]

Ronald C. Pilenzo, president of the Society for Human Resource Management, said:

> You still have to be a team member, but what's wrong with being the best possible team member and still being noticed at the same time?[3]

Ross Webber, a professor of management at the University of Pennsylvania's Wharton School, answered:

> I think personal career development and being a team player are compatible if you accept your interdependence with other people. If you are going to influence them, they have got to be able to influence you. You must have the courage to be honest with other people in communicating your desires and concerns.[4]

David L. Bradford, a lecturer in organizational behavior at the Stanford Graduate School of Business and coauthor of *Influence Without Authority* (John Wiley & Sons Inc.) said:

> You can certainly use an individual advancement program and still be a team player. One important managerial skill is, ''How do I balance my own needs with the needs of the department and the organization?'' If any one of them becomes dominant, then parties lose out.[5]

Dan Murphy, president of Corporate Dynamics, answered:

> Office politics does not have to have a negative connotation. Office politics can be played in order to foster team spirit and help the organization arrive at its objectives.[6]

When others in the business community read about you in the press, they often believe that your career is on the fast track. While publicity is good for you, it is also good for the company. Company officials like to see the company name in print almost as much as you enjoy seeing your own name. Always clear your press releases and articles with the personnel or public relations office.

Write Articles for Trade or Business Journals.   Companies often perceive that someone who writes an article for a business publication is an authority on the subject. As a result, they fight for these people and pay them well because having an authority on the payroll adds prestige to their organizations.

The funny thing about this is that the people who write these articles usually are not the best authorities on the topic. They simply had the discipline to sit down and write an article.

Build clout for yourself by asking the editors of a publication if they would be interested in an idea you have for an article. Keep submitting different ideas until a publication accepts one of your proposals.

Talk to Outside Organizations.   Contact the club president or the person who is in charge of scheduling programs for group meetings to suggest a program they might enjoy. Make sure your presentation is polished because the audience will judge you by your program. Pass out literature about your company. Bring a stack of business cards.

KNOW WHEN TO RISK YOUR JOB FOR YOUR PRINCIPLES

Stand up for a wronged co-worker? Speak up against an unpopular office policy? Make sure it's worth it. The result can be disastrous. You lose clout or perhaps your job simply because you picked the wrong battle to fight.

But there are occasions, and thankfully they are few, when you find you cannot passively tolerate a situation or decision. You might find yourself facing a painful choice: your job or your principles.

So what do you do? Quit? Speak up? Remain neutral?

In such cases, there are no easy answers. You have to trust your instincts.

Ask yourself: What are the consequences of speaking up? Will you lose clout? Will the boss make *you* the next target? Will you end up in the unemployment line?

Now ask yourself: Is it really worth sacrificing your job for your principles?

If it is, speak up.

If it isn't, keep your mouth shut. And remind yourself:
There are times in every worker's life when the boss says, "Two plus two equals six," and you agree. (What if the boss wants you to do something illegal or unethical? See Chapter 5.)

HOW TO TAP THE OFFICE GRAPEVINE

You need to tap the office grapevine. There is much information management might not tell you that you need to know. Unanticipated changes in personnel, policy, or organization can affect your career.

Are you rubbing someone the wrong way? Who has the inside track for a job promotion? Is a big policy change in the works? Who is going to be the new boss? What is the new boss like? Is the company considering a merger? Keeping abreast of what is happening gives you an edge when planning your tactics. Take a journalistic approach and cultivate multiple sources that can provide you with advanced warning about changes that can affect your job.

Often sources don't like to give you information unless they get a little information in return. The best thing to do is repeat old news. And keep the good scoops to yourself.

Possible sources could be peers and outside competitors. Secretaries can also be an information bonanza. After all, who answers the telephone, sits in on meetings, and types correspondence going out of the office? Especially make friends with the secretary in the personnel office.

''I think people enjoy the camaraderie of sharing information that is privy to themselves,'' says Peter Kurth, a human resources executive with Barnett Bank. ''It is a way of saying to someone, 'Hey, I trust you, I'm your friend.' ''[7]

A study sponsored by Robert Half International shows that 80 to 85 percent of what people discuss off the cuff at the water cooler has some basis in fact.[8] But you need to dig deeper. You need to know which gossip is incomplete or erroneous.

Here is a conversation that illustrates a subtle way to get information without getting a reputation as an office gossip.
Two employees exchange information after a firing:

INEPT OFFICE POLITICIAN

I can't believe what a complete idiot Tom is for firing Diane.

SAVVY OFFICE POLITICIAN
What do you think about Diane?

Smart office politicians learn how to gather information discreetly without developing reputations as office gossips. They know that their mission is to gather information about business operations and not to trash someone's personal life. They do it with class by gathering facts and gently prompting their sources to talk further.

When you exchange information with a source, try not to spice up the conversation with your personal opinion. During an exchange, avoid revealing your opinion about a change or how you plan to react to it.

Regardless of how you feel about something that occurs at the office, don't say anything that you would not want to get back to everyone in your office, including your boss, supervisor, or co-worker.

In the previous example, the boss would probably not be too angry if some of his employees discussed Diane's firing, but he certainly would not take kindly to being called an idiot.

AVOID DATING ANYONE WHO WORKS IN YOUR DEPARTMENT

All of us know people who have met their spouses at work and have lived happily ever after.

Yet, some unromantic statistics suggest that many office love affairs end badly. More than 40 percent of the people who responded to my survey believe dating a boss or co-workers is a mistake. Another 33 percent believe that you should avoid dating a boss or co-worker, or at least date someone in another department. Surprisingly, only 6 percent of people surveyed felt dating at work doesn't create any problems for the people involved.

With statistics like that, you have to ask yourself if dating someone from your office is going to enhance your life significantly. Do you believe that the possibility of marrying your office love justifies the risk of career stagnation, changing jobs, or even getting fired?

If you honestly feel that you can't live without the other person, you must consider the risks at hand. Careers have been derailed by relationships that have gone sour.

Don't delude yourself into believing that if you're discreet, you won't experience any adverse consequences. Some employees have left jobs because they could not cope with working alongside a former lover. Your career can stall because of allegations of favoritism. Sexual harassment suits can also be brought by ex-lovers.

It can also be quite embarrassing to work with an ex-lover who might blab the intimate details of your sex life to other co-workers. Stories about impotence, nymphomania, pornography, and fetishes, true or not, can have disastrous career consequences should they become public knowledge around the office. Many people have been fired or forced to quit because their former lovers don't want to see them around the office anymore.

It usually doesn't take long for your co-workers to recognize two people having an office love affair. They are not oblivious to the

---

TACTIC

How to Turn a Boss or Co-Worker Down for a Date

"I think the best way to turn down a date from the boss is to say, 'I'm involved,' whether you are or not," says Thomas L. Quick, executive director of Resource Strategies Institute, and author of 20 management books.[9]

It's usually not a good idea to say, "I'm sorry, but I've got other plans." If your boss persists in asking you out, you may run out of excuses.

Here are some ways to turn a boss down for a date:

- Thank you, but I've got a special person.
- I'm flattered, but I don't date people I work with.
- Thank you. I'd love to, but I never mix business with pleasure.
- I'm involved.
- I appreciate your interest, but a personal relationship isn't compatible with our business relationship.

---

body language and romantic looks that a couple having an office romance exchange.

Eventually, upper management also becomes aware of an office romance and may view it unfavorably. This is especially true if any of the parties involved are married. Management wants trustworthy people who have the respect of their peers and co-workers. Upper management has been known to promote less qualified employees over those who are in the midst of a relationship. They don't like to promote people who are the butt of office jokes and rumors.

Take it from Marie, 38, an administrative assistant with a major hotel chain:

> I dated my boss. It was disastrous. He was a career man who had many years in the company. After six months of dating, we became engaged.
>
> Our company did not allow two people within the same department to be married. So, I went to management and said, "We set a wedding date, and I'd like to transfer to another department."

They did not like how my fiance had been behaving as a supervisor. They decided to punish him by not giving me a transfer.

I resigned. Then he broke our engagement. I was out a career and a husband. I made myself a rule. I will never again date anyone from work.

Better yet, listen to 30-year-old Nancy, who dated one of her subordinates, then spent two years in a state of humiliation:

> To make a long story short, he dumped me after a year of living together. He acted like he was being so discreet, but everyone knew what had happened. Everyone knew how I had made a fool out of myself when he broke up with me. Everyone sided with him.
>
> He continued to report to me and I had to make a big deal about how objective I was about his work. I hated him. I felt like everyone was laughing at me. People gossiped about us for more than a year. Then he started dating this brainless nymph in our office, and everyone was watching my reaction.
>
> Guess what? He married her. I felt so used. But I finally got another job and left. I thought I had learned my lesson, but I'm dating another man in my office. Who knows, maybe this time it will work out.

DON'T BE INTIMIDATED BY A DIFFICULT BOSS OR CO-WORKER

You also need to develop a winning strategy to outwit an unfair boss or co-worker. Despite efforts by some players to shatter your self-confidence, you must always fight to maintain it. Keep your self-confidence high by refusing to let them intimidate you. A useful strategy is to try to act rather than react to your challenges.

Office emperors are hungry for a power fix. They enjoy intimidating subordinates who must do whatever they tell them to do. Such overlords are demeaning, insulting, demanding, manipulative, and difficult to work for.

Publicly you must project an attitude of loyalty and support for the values of your company and boss. Don't give an unfair boss the satisfaction of knowing that he intimidates you. Use the same confident attitude to handle difficult co-workers.

TACTIC

How to Fend Off an Oral Attack

Here are some responses to counter an attack by an offensive boss:

- I can understand why you might feel that way.
- Why did you ask that question?
- If I were you, I would feel the exact same way.
- I think you already know the answer to that question.
- Let us talk about . . . instead.
- What would you do if you were me?
- Oh, by the way . . .

Consider this example:

Scott, the Shoe Store Manager.   Scott was in trouble. The boss was in town and he was angry. ''For the past year,'' he said, ''sales have stunk.''

''I am shocked by how mediocre your sales figures were this year,'' said the district manager. ''When Doug was manager of this store, it was the top store in the region. I don't know what you did to make sales decline so much. How come all the other stores in my region had sales increases except yours? How could you let sales drop 18 percent in one year? Your display windows are unattractive. Why do you keep the stockroom such a mess?''

Scott just sat there and took his boss's verbal abuse. He didn't have to. Scott could have neutralized his boss' attack on him.

Scott should have said, ''I know sales were not up to par this year. It is going to be a big challenge to increase them, but I'm ready for that challenge. What would you do to meet that challenge?''

His boss probably would have discussed positive ideas such as advertising, displays, and price strategy. Regardless of his competence, Scott could have changed the tone of the conversation with one smart question.

Don't sit still if you are on the wrong end of an unfair attack. Recognize exactly what the other person is trying to do. Ask yourself if you honestly deserve the beating. If the answer is no, ask the other person a couple of questions that can often change a negative conversation into a more positive one.

DON'T BLAB YOUR STRATEGIES TO YOUR CO-WORKERS

Your co-workers may not be your most loyal supporters. While most will hope you succeed on the job, they would rather be the ones on the receiving end of a promotion or salary increase.

By all means collaborate, go bowling, play golf, join the lunch group, and exchange quips with your rivals. Just don't make the mistake of getting too buddy-buddy with them.

The competitive nature of work often precludes you from having the same type of close friendships that you have outside of work. When you tell co-workers things that increase your prestige in the company, you risk incurring their wrath and their jealousy.

Resist sharing your feelings, goals, and sensitive opinions with co-workers who might use the information against you. Some insecure co-workers may steal, minimize, or lobby against you or your ideas if they want to maintain the status quo.

Consider this example:

Greg and Sam are attorneys in a medium-sized law firm. They have equal rank and equal seniority. Their boss retires. Either Greg or Sam will get his job, a $22,000 pay increase, and a sure shot at partnership.

Greg wants it. Sam desperately needs it. He's got a new baby on the way and is already drowning in his debts.

They are good friends. But with the boss's retirement, it is critical that they keep their strategies to themselves. Telling too much to a competitor is a sure way to lose the edge.

Greg shouldn't tell Sam his plans for restructuring the trust department if he's selected. He also shouldn't tell Sam that he declined a job offer from a competing law firm last week. Nor should Sam frustrate

Greg by boasting how he just brought the firm three new clients and has just published an article in a nationally distributed legal magazine.

Sharing sensitive information could tempt one man to increase his chance of promotion at the expense of the other. For example, Sam could disarm his competition by saying to his managing partner, "I probably shouldn't be saying this but I'm concerned about the backlog of work that would develop if Greg takes the job at the competing law firm." Sam could also gain influence by trying to pass off Greg's ideas for restructuring the department as his own.

Greg could also feel threatened by Sam's coup in client development and start bad-mouthing Sam to his superiors. Greg could do this by showing some of Sam's deficient work and revealing stories about disloyalty.

Competition is a natural part of the workplace. Recognize it. Deal with it. Use it. But don't give another employee the ammunition needed to trample you in the process.

DECIDE WHAT YOUR COMPANY WANTS YOU TO BE, AND BE IT

Part of your job is learning the things that management expects from you. Many of these things aren't shown on your job description. Here are three attributes essential to career advancement:

Loyalty.   Always show your willingness to achieve company goals. That willingness to help has allowed many a marginal employee to outwit or postpone the ax.

Even if you work for a second-rate organization, act as if you love working for the company. Make your superiors believe that you are happy to be part of such a dynamic organization. You can do this by acting in an enthusiastic and supportive manner.

Always try to make your boss look good in the organization. Help your boss to avoid a costly mistake. If your boss plans to spend thousands of dollars on a computer system that is practically obsolete, tell him about the technological advances of another system that he might not be familiar with. He will probably thank you for saving his hide.

Don't spread remarks that could do your boss damage throughout the company. Loyalty to a boss is mandatory. Dissension is rarely tolerated.

While you might not always agree with your superiors, let them know that you are not going to create any problems for them. You have to publicly support management.

Productivity. Employers want employees who generate revenue, not overhead. Salespeople are judged by how much they sell. Professionals are judged by the number of workhours they have billed to clients.

Consider the case of two attorneys who earn $35,000 a year. With benefits, it costs the firm $39,179 to keep them on the payroll. Their time is billed out at $50 an hour.

At the end of the year, Lawyer A has 1,420 chargeable hours, and Lawyer B has 1,845 chargeable hours. Based strictly on productivity, Lawyer A is in trouble. Here's why:

Lawyer A		
1,420 hours worked × $50 per hour		$71,000
Less expenses:		
Salary and benefits	$39,179	
Share of firm overhead	30,000	
	$69,179	69,179
Profit made by attorney A for the firm		$1,821
Lawyer B		
1,845 hours worked × $50 per hour		$92,250
Less expenses:		
Salary and benefits	$39,179	
Share of firm overhead	30,000	
	$69,179	69,179
Profit made by attorney B for the firm		$23,071

The partners of the firm can't help being impressed with B's job performance. Since the firm barely broke even with lawyer A's performance this year, they are not likely to offer him a salary increase. Lawyer B generated extra revenue for the firm; she should be eligible for a salary increase. If A's productivity does not improve, he could be dropped from the firm in favor of someone who generates more revenue.

Now you know the importance of productivity. Here are some suggestions to improve yours.

How to be More Productive for Your Company

- Guard against daydreaming. Daydreaming 15 minutes each workday accumulates into approximately 65 hours of unproductive time a year.
- If you don't know how to do something, don't waste time spinning your wheels. You will save a lot of time by asking someone who knows how to do the task rather than getting frustrated in a effort to teach yourself. Ask enough questions of a knowledgeable superior or co-worker until you know how to complete the assignment.
- Procrastination is brutal to productivity because it can snowball into mediocrity. Conquer procrastination by performing your tasks as soon as possible. You don't have to waste time worrying about a task that you've already completed.
- Always make a written list of the things you want to do each day. The things you don't have a chance to complete should be shown on tomorrow's list. Each day, break down your list into the things that you must do, should do, and could do. You should establish priorities for each item on your list. Assign high priorities to the less pleasant activities.
- Take a time-management course.
- Do things right the first time. Don't waste time doing something over that should have been done properly the first time.
- Determine what you are trying to do. Plan how to do it. Then do it.
- Don't waste time looking for things. Keep your office, files, and work area well-organized throughout your workday.

- If you are not going to make a deadline, keep your boss informed about your progress. He may extend your deadline or assign some of your co-workers to help you out.
- Learn how to become more efficient at your job. Perhaps something that you are doing could be done better by a secretary or computer.

Offer New Ideas and Take the Initiative. Don't make the mistake of waiting for additional responsibilities or projects to fall into your lap. Make the first move by asking your boss for new duties.

Management doesn't want you to go through your job duties on autopilot. Employers always want you to think constantly about what you can do to perform your duties more efficiently.

Without being intimidating, tell your boss your ideas about how you can save the company money, increase department productivity, or offer clients better service. There is one definite advantage to suggesting a desirable idea or plan to management: Chances are that you will be the one who gets to investigate or carry out the idea or plan.

Beth Walch, 26, tells how she made the jump from assistant buyer to buyer at Beall's Department Stores once she heard that there was an opening. She was not in line for the promotion; she lacked seniority and credentials. But she had initiative.

I lobbied for my position as a buyer in a very centered way. Even before I found out about the opening, I let my boss know and her boss know that if an opening came up, I would be interested in it. I had to express my interest because I feared that I might get passed over, again.

When an opening came up, I wrote a letter to the vice president of merchandising saying that I heard there was an opening in sportswear and I wanted the job. I then listed everything that I had done in the past year that was exemplary.

Later, I went in and asked the vice president if he had any questions. One week later, I went in and asked him if he had filled the position yet. I then told him that I wanted to be formally interviewed.

I got the job. I learned that if I wanted something, I had to let someone know that I was interested.[10]

TIP

Position Yourself for Promotion

"Get yourself ready either through experience or education. Then position yourself so that when a job becomes available, you become the leading candidate. This is the best way to get promoted," says Ronald C. Pilenzo.[11]

Sure, Beth could have been turned down. But by taking the initiative, she got a jump on her competition before the position was advertised to outsiders or posted on the company bulletin board.

The central principle here is that you must recognize that there is more to career success than logging long hours.

ADDICTED TO WORK—ARE YOU AT RISK?

Some managers lose direction in life by becoming overly devoted company people or terminal workaholics. They miss opportunities to enjoy their families and participate in satisfying nonwork activities. Sadly, these people place a premium on career success even if their home life suffers as a result.

Ironically, these company men and women believe that they are irreplaceable. If, by chance, they should die in the prime of life, companies can usually replace them quickly.

What if you start a new job and notice that your co-workers work from 8 A.M. to 7 P.M., even though official hours are 9 to 5? In all likelihood, the boss wants employees that are committed to the company. You can't afford to be an exception. But you don't have to work three hours of unpaid overtime each day, either.

You might consider coming to work at 7:30 in the morning. Let people think that you've been on the job since sunrise. Even if you don't plan to do any work, consider taking a briefcase home with you each night. Your boss won't know that you didn't open the briefcase and spent the night watching television with your family.

You need to communicate to your boss through your behavior that you are enthusiastic and committed to the organization. You don't want your boss to stereotype you as a clockwatcher, only interested in collecting a paycheck. Smart office politicians learn how to act like company men and women without neglecting, within reason, their health and families.

MAKE YOURSELF INDISPENSABLE

Doing well may help you survive in even the most turbulent office environments. Good salespeople have more rights than bad salespeople. Good planners have more rights than bad planners.

Job security is a fringe benefit. The more you make your boss look good, the more secure your job is. Remember, a boss is less likely to fire you if you were partly responsible for her bonus.

The Wall Street Journal once reported the results of a study that asked secretaries, "What does a good secretary do for the boss?" One secretary replied, "I do everything except breathe and go to the bathroom for him." Her humorous answer provides a valuable defense to office politics: Make yourself indispensable.

PLAY THE GAME THE COMPANY'S WAY

Companies do things for a reason. Right or wrong, you have to guard against a common baby boomer tendency of saying, "Why should I do it this way?" or "Isn't there a better way?" Instead, say "Yes, I'm going to do it."

Many baby boomers have found it difficult or almost impossible to change the policy at some companies. John Stacy, who left his job as a management trainee at Barnett Bank, says, "I was told that I was too impatient because I suggested that Barnett take a more aggressive commercial loan strategy."[12]

When you are the low person on the company totem pole, you often can't change the company policy until you control it.

R. Wayne Smith, 35, a veteran branch manager with Barnett Bank, plays the game the way his bosses want him to play it.

As a middle manager, part of my job and the way that I perceive my job is being the yes man. I don't make policy for the bank. I am asked to carry out policy for the bank. I am asked for my opinion on certain policies or certain ways Barnett should do things based on my field experience.

In the final analysis, I don't make those decisions, so to some degree I must follow rules, policies, and procedures.

My job as a middle manager is to take what is given to me and communicate it to the staff and the client in a positive manner.[13]

TIP

How to Make Yourself Indispensable

- Be the master of a task that no one else in the office knows how to do. For example, be the Lotus 1-2-3 authority in a department where the boss just knows how to turn the computer on.
- Prove your worth. Think of ways to save the company money, and attract new clients.
- Volunteer to do work that is not getting done in your department.
- Emphasize your desire to help the company, management, and people in your department to get things done more efficiently.
- Make sure the boss can count on you to make him look good with his bosses.
- Subtly let your firm know that the major clients like you. The implication here is that the company might lose clients if you opened your own firm.
- Always increase your professional skills and improve your abilities. The more you know and the more duties you can perform, the more valuable you are to the company.

I agree with Wayne. A big part of entry-level and management positions is following company policy. Remember, most companies expect you to follow policy and not to make or change it. If you want to change a policy, make sure that you follow the rules for changing that policy.

AT A GLANCE

Use the rules of office politics to help you protect your job, cope with a difficult boss, manage your co-workers, and get your dream job.

The rules can also help you survive in an office that doesn't reward the most qualified worker.

While following these rules and strategies is not 100 percent foolproof, your chances for achieving career success can improve greatly.

The Rules of Office Politics

1. Impress the people who have the power to advance your career.
2. Know when to risk your job for your principles.
3. Tap the office grapevine.
4. Avoid having a relationship with a boss or coworker in your department.
5. Don't be intimidated by a difficult boss or coworker.
6. Don't blab your strategies to your co-workers.
7. Decide what your company wants you to be, and be it.
8. Don't be a work addict.
9. Make yourself indispensable.
10. Play the game the company's way.

CHAPTER 2   AUTHOR INTERVIEWS

1. Ronald C. Pilenzo, May 18, 1990.
2. Thomas R. Horton, May 21, 1990.
3. Pilenzo, May 18, 1990.
4. Ross Webber, May 21, 1990.
5. David L. Bradford, May 21, 1990.
6. Dan Murphy, May 16, 1990.
7. Peter Kurth, June 22, 1988.
8. Robert Half, June 8, 1988.
9. Thomas L. Quick, May 15, 1990.
10. Beth Walch, April 26, 1988.
11. Pilenzo, May 18, 1990.
12. John Stacy, August 23, 1988.
13. R. Wayne Smith, June 1, 1988.

Chapter Three

How to Win Friends and Influence Baby Boomers

O n paper, you may have it all: an MBA and Phi Beta Kappa at a top university.

One problem, though. When it comes to saying all the right things to all the right people, you choke. Like thousands of talented, intelligent people, you lack one element needed for success: a winning personality.

Today, a bad personality costs you money and success. Consider these casualties from the work front:

Tom, 36, a gifted but introverted engineer, missed a big promotion. Management chose a more personable employee who could lead group meetings, even though Tom was a better engineer.

Maggie, 26, an ambitious, capable MBA, seemed to have it all. Too bad she let her competence and winning ways intimidate her boss; he thought she wanted his job. To save his hide, he torpedoed Maggie with bad assignments and quotas. He got what he wanted: Maggie quit.

Don, 30, a financial analyst, doesn't know why his co-workers lobby against his business plans and ideas. Well, Don, it's your ethnic and sexual remarks like, ''Of course you'd think that—you're Jewish.''

Indeed, human relations can be your downfall. Simply working hard and knowing a lot is no guarantee of a place at the top. There *is* no shortage of people in gray suits who can do your job.

But there is a shortage of people who exude leadership, enthusiasm, and energy. Usually, those who do, have long, prosperous careers.

The secret of their success? They know how to build and maintain good relations with co-workers, bosses, and clients.

Unfortunately, "most people are not building the quality professional relationships they should be building at work," says Elwood Chapman.[1] Chapman is the author of *Your Attitude Is Showing* (Science Research Associates).

"You may have majored in engineering or computer science because you need those skills to get your first job," says Thomas R. Horton, chairman and CEO of the American Management Association. "But if you want to get up the ladder, those aren't the skills you need. You need human relations skills."[2]

To get ahead, you must show your boss you can:

- Work well with people at all levels.
- Inspire, motivate, and persuade others.
- Win support for your business plans and ideas.
- Change attitudes without making enemies.
- Hobnob with movers and shakers.
- Make successful sales pitches.
- Butter up existing clients.
- Drum up new business.

One bone of contention: Not only are those skills not taught in college, but they're usually not taught at work, either. That's why people pay thousands of dollars to buy a new personality from Dale Carnegie & Associates and scores of other motivational gurus.

Save your money. You probably don't need a high-priced speaking and human relations course to get those skills. There's another way.

High-caliber human relations skills are taught in this chapter. Use the different strategies and tactics to: (1) work well with bosses, (2) handle co-workers and clients, (3) make yourself more persuasive, (4) cultivate a good business personality, (5) gain self-confidence, and (6) turn human relation skills into money and success.

HUMAN RELATIONS STRATEGIES FOR THE 90s

Here's your ticket to the top:

1. Make your boss work for you.
2. Make the first move.
3. Be sincere.
4. Greet your co-workers every day.
5. Offer a helping hand.
6. Don't be stingy with praise.
7. Make yourself persuasive.
8. Nobody wins an argument, but . . . .
9. Don't be a schlemiel.
10. Pay attention.

MAKE YOUR BOSS WORK FOR YOU

No matter where you are on the company ladder, you will always have a boss. It is, perhaps, the one universal of the workplace.

Bosses can promote you or demote you. They can hire you or fire you. They can give you a raise or give you an ulcer.

That's why you need to learn how to make your boss work for you. At stake is your happiness and future career advancement.

By all means, let your boss think he's superboss. Just use human relations training to get him to do what you want him to do.

Marcy, a newspaper reporter, told me:

My supervisor was constantly checking me. She was always interrupting me and telling me how to write stories. She was also obsessed with trying to find out who my sources were.

I'm no kid right out of journalism school. I've got more than 10 years experience and a master's degree to boot.

Perhaps she was intimidated by my competence and qualifications—hers couldn't compare.

So instead of waiting for her to check up on me, I'd tell her exactly what I was doing. I informed her who I was interviewing. And more important, I stroked her ego by asking good questions even though I already knew the answers.

Later, she stopped smothering me. You see, I reassured her that she was necessary.

Here are some ways to make your boss work for you:

Try Not to be Best Friends with a Boss. These relationships seem so natural because you likely have much in common. But befriending a superior is often a mistake. You have plenty to lose. Your boss may try so hard not to give preferential treatment to you that he or she is extra tough on a daily basis. In the long term, you might miss a promotion.

Any trouble in your personal relationship may find its way into the office. If you have personal problems with your boss, you will likely suffer at work. You may think you have more power than

When you go above the boss's head, make sure the gain is worth the gamble.

TIP

Going above the Boss's Head

"There are many reasons to go above a boss's head," says Thomas L. Quick, executive director of Resource Strategies Institute. "But you have to realize once you do so, you may have very well destroyed your relationship with your immediate boss."[4]

Make sure the gain is worth the gamble. "When you say, Hey, I'm going over the boss's head,' you have to be able to understand that it's a last ditch resort. There may be no recourse after that. You may get what you want, but you probably will pay a hell of a price," says Quick.[5]

---

you have because of your friendship with the boss. Also, your co-workers will probably resent you.

Remember, bosses should not know too much about you. Nor should they worry that you know too much about them.

Keep your boss primed, but as a bowling partner—not a confidante or psychiatrist.

Some Days Will Be Hell. There will be some days a boss may jump on you unfairly. You don't like it, of course you don't. Unfortunately, you can't let your boss's mood swings affect your job performance.

Sometimes you will be hounded because your performance is not up to snuff. But realize that sometimes you will be hounded because *your boss's* performance is being scrutinized.

Bosses can be moody, and it is important to try to determine what their moods are about. Don't flatter yourself into thinking every nasty look and smart remark is directed only at you.

Don't Let a Legitimate Gripe Fester. When things bother you, accept the status quo or do something about it.

TACTIC

How to Speak to a Boss Who Doesn't Know What He's Talking about.

Most bosses mean well, but on occasion they have incredibly stupid ideas.

Suppose you're in a big staff meeting and the big boss says, ''I'm thinking about changing all employees from a one-hour lunch to a half-hour lunch. The company can save close to $90,000 a year.'' His idea is a loser, a megadog. When it comes to productivity, declines in employee morale would be catastrophic. And the cost savings are just not worth it.

OK, the negatives makes you sick. Should you express an opinion contrary to the boss, perhaps rubbing the boss the wrong way? Or keep quiet and witness Armageddon around the office?

**How to Speak Up at a Staff Meeting
Without Ticking Off the Boss**

Your Response	Likely Result	Price to Pay
You're crazy!	More negative entries in your personnel file	Depends on boss's personality—anything from a nasty look to making your life miserable
Silence	No short-term consequences	Are you a fixture or management material?
With all due respect to your opinion . . .	You rub boss the wrong way	Boss might not respect someone who rambles
That's fantastic!	Your job is secure	Boss and co-workers know you are a brownnoser
Have you considered . . . ? What would happen if?	You score points on style	None—boss knows you're diplomatic

What are your chief goals in making this decision?	Shows you think before you react	None—boss knows you're loyal
Tell idea to supervisor first; let supervisor decide whether to discuss idea with boss	Cautious approach—supervisor relays winners and trashes losers.	Supervisor may steal credit for your good idea
Voice disagreement in written memo later	Rules for writing are same as speaking	Boss appreciates that you didn't embarrass him in front of a group
Here's how I see it: The pros are . . . The cons are . . .	You gain nothing—you haven't revealed where you stand and you look gutless	Boss may think you're a wimp

Either way, you don't want to let something that annoys you affect your morale. The best way to handle this is to talk to your supervisor. Once it's resolved, you can forget about it and get back to normal.

Timing Is Essential. Smart workers learn to pick the right time to talk with a supervisor. When a boss has a monumental deadline, it's pure suicide to voice your concerns. Postpone discussing your concerns until she has the time to talk.

Get Human Relations Training. "Most people feel human relations is something you are born with," says Elwood Chapman. "They might feel they don't have to take training in it. And they underestimate it."[3] Don't make the same mistake; human relations skills are essential if you want a successful business career.

Don't Be Afraid of Your Supervisor. He's your supervisor, not God. Bad supervisors might be unethical, harass you, or promote pets who shouldn't be promoted.

Don't be so afraid of a boss that you can't stand reasonable ground, or at least voice an opinion. While you should not normally go above a supervisor's head, there are times you may have to do just that. (We're not talking office misdemeanors here.)

Some bosses need to be kept in line so they don't victimize you. If that means talking with personnel, talk with personnel. If it means asking for a transfer, ask for a transfer. Even if you have to resign (hopefully, that won't be necessary), you don't want to let a boss demean you.

MAKE THE FIRST MOVE

Human beings fear rejection. Take making new friends and business contacts, for example.

Most Chambers of Commerce now have a Business After Hours. Business After Hours is a huge cocktail party, usually held after work hours where you can promote yourself and your company in a relaxed social setting.

At a Business After Hours, people usually stand around like wallflowers. They wait for someone to walk up to them and start a conversation.

Often, they feel too paralyzed to walk up to a stranger and say, "Hi, I'm . . . How do you like this event?" They fear if they make the first move, someone might say, "You nerd, how dare you come up to me?" or, "Excuse me, there is a cheese doodle with my name on it."

When I go to a Business After Hours, I make the first move. Yes, I go up to complete strangers and initiate a conversation. Have I ever been rebuffed for a cheese doodle? Of course not.

Instead, most people are thrilled to be sought out. They appreciate that I made the first move. Why? Since they have someone to talk to, they no longer feel like wallflowers.

That, in a nutshell, is why you must force yourself to make the first move. You don't have to be a great conversationalist to do this. Just introduce yourself. Then ask a couple of probing questions. (See the list of 25 questions to spark conversation in Chapter 4.) From there, you can talk business or friendship.

TACTIC

Cultivate the New Kid on the Block

Don't get in the rut of always going to lunch with the same people each day. Sure, you enjoy their company, but you also limit exposure to new friends and business contacts.

Avoid getting into or promoting cliques in your office. An office is a nicer place to work when people work in harmony.

Act congenially to new employees. Make an effort to introduce them around the company and make sure they have someone to eat lunch with. You might tell them the boss's likes and dislikes. They will appreciate your effort.

Outside work, ask potential clients and other people you would like to network with out to lunch or out for a drink. Don't let cost stop you from doing this. One rule of the career jungle is that when you buy someone a free lunch, they pick up the tab next time.

Remember to make the first move. You'll make more friends, get more invitations, and drum up more business.

BE SINCERE

I remember feeling a little lonely when I moved to Sarasota, Florida, to accept a position with a large regional accounting firm. Since I was new to the area, I hadn't met many people.

One night at an open house for a new law firm, I met Robert, a young stockbroker, who seemed friendly, and we exchanged business cards.

The next day Robert called me at my office and asked me to go to lunch. It pleased me to think that he wanted to go to lunch with me because he wanted to establish a friendship with me.

We ordered lunch at a downtown restaurant. He then asked me for the names of all my clients. He wanted to sell them securities so he could earn big commission checks. When I told Robert that it was against firm policy to give him the names of clients, he became very upset with me. His demeanor became more unpleasant by the minute as he pressured me to introduce him to the firm's partners and professional staff. He wanted to make their acquaintance to push his stocks and bonds. I declined to introduce him to the firm, paid for my own lunch, and left with a valuable lesson.

I learned firsthand how lousy it feels to be used by someone. I had erroneously thought the stockbroker wanted me for a friend, but his sole purpose was to use me to prospect clients.

As a result of his lunch performance, he would never have an opportunity to know me any better. The only thing the stockbroker wanted from me was to take.

The message here should be that people will be more responsive to you when you treat them well. Don't be like the stockbroker. Show them you care.

When you care about people, they are more likely to choose you for a friend, associate, or business partner. Moral: Just be sincere and natural.

GREET YOUR CO-WORKERS EVERY DAY

Now, let's take a look at one of the biggest human relations traps for entry-level people.

"I think my biggest problem when I came to Coast Federal Savings and Loan was my shyness," says Veronica Booth, 24, an assistant treasurer. "I was thrown into a brand-new setting where I didn't know if people wanted to talk to me.

"There were people at all levels of the company that I would give a shy smile or say, 'Hi.' Unfortunately, some people thought I was a snob because I wasn't overly friendly. Not true—I was just shy.

"In retrospect, I should have got my guts up and gone in and said, 'Hi, I'm Veronica Booth,' and shaken hands. I should have forced myself to put on a cocktail party attitude and say hi to everyone."[6]

Learn from Veronica. Go out of your way to greet your co-

TACTIC

How to Get New Clients

People who are good at client development rise quickly in any organization. They're pure fast track for a reason: They generate lots of extra revenue for their companies.

To be sure, not everyone can hustle clients. It takes talent, intelligence, and style.

Here's how to score new clients:

- Ask potential clients out for lunch or a drink after work. People appreciate these inexpensive gestures of goodwill; they can be a gold mine for new clients.
- Dazzle potential clients with technical competence. How? Entice them by giving free samples; answer their questions with confidence, accuracy, and style.
- Treat current clients well. When they're happy, they send referrals.
- Prospect. Prospect. Remember, every person you meet is a potential client or can refer you to a client.
- Join civic, athletic, and religious groups to expose yourself to possible clients.
- Don't be a social misfit. People often judge competence by how you conduct yourself socially.
- Ask for referrals. Ask people if they know others you could help.
- Give speeches and seminars to the "right" groups. (Ask participants to fill in data cards so you can contact them later.)
- Direct mail and telemarketing are expensive but can provide valuable leads.
- Make a lasting impression. Your professional image sets the tone for future business dealings.
- Pass out lots of business cards. If your company won't spring for cards, buy them yourself. They're cheap and great advertising (less than $30 for 1,000 business cards).

workers. Make yourself an easier person to meet and deal with. The result? You'll have fewer problems dealing with co-workers and you'll have a happier work environment.

Here are a few tips to make it easy for people to like you.

- Greet your co-workers everyday. Use simple but effective greetings like, "Good Morning," "Hi," "How are you feeling?" and "How was your weekend?"
- Act friendly. Whether someone works in the mailroom or is a vice president, smile, shake hands, wave, or nod your head. You can never have too many allies.
- Ask co-workers out to lunch. (Separate checks are the norm.)
- Take part in company-sponsored activities such as softball games, bowling leagues, and picnics.

OFFER A HELPING HAND

Yes, sometimes it's a dog-eat-dog world. And yes, there are sleazy reptiles who might play up to the boss at your expense. But most bosses and co-workers are sincere people who just want to do their jobs.

"You can be a barracuda and skip from one job to another and maybe even crawl to the top a little, but you don't have good relationships along the way," says Elwood Chapman. "There has to be a mutual reward in any good relationship."[7]

Remember Chapter 1? Yes, that's right—all that New Breed stuff about people who are reluctant to seek help. In particular, many New Breeders are afraid to let people know they're floundering.

Hmmm . . . Do you see a big opportunity here? You can win these people over easily. Just show them you're a nice person and not some sleazy reptile.

How? By being a helper.

Fact: When you help people, they usually respond favorably to you. What's more, you build a more harmonious work environment for yourself.

If you see someone struggling at work, come to his rescue. Show him shortcuts. Train him. Offer help. And yes, tip him off if he's in trouble with the boss.

And if someone needs to pick up her car in the shop, give her a ride. Or if a co-worker is in the hospital, send a cheery get well card. Those are just a few examples, to point you in the right direction.

In no one way am I saying you have to offer every person you meet your last dollar. *Just be a decent person.* Because the person you help today just might save your hide tomorrow.

DON'T BE STINGY WITH PRAISE

"I've seen a lot of superstar engineers come and go at Florida Power and Light," says Ty Ross, a training specialist. "Right off the bat, I can see the ones who are going to have problems. They might be geniuses as engineers, but if they irritate people, they're not going to be effective.

"Take dealing with secretaries, for instance. I've seen engineers create enemies by saying, 'Hurry up and type this letter for me; I'm in a real rush'; or 'God, it's about time.'

"But if you ask the right way, there isn't a thing a secretary at FP&L won't do for you. You fare better with remarks like: 'You know, I really like the way you did this,' 'I appreciate the good job you did for me,' or 'This looks very good, just the way I wanted it. Thanks a lot,'" says Ross.[8]

What does this mean for you? For starters, to be successful, you must work well with people at *all* levels in your company.

That is where giving *sincere* praise fits in. Only when you make someone feel important and appreciated can you hope to gain that person's cooperation and friendship. Perhaps the quickest way to do this is to give plenty of sincere praise.

So take it from Mark Twain, who once said, "I can live for two months on a good compliment." If Twain felt so good, imagine how your co-workers will respond.*

The New Lexicon Webster's Dictionary of the English Language (New York: Lexicon Publications, Inc., 1988), PP. QD-73.

MAKE YOURSELF MORE PERSUASIVE

What do Madison Avenue, your spouse, and your boss have in common? Answer: They are masters of persuasion.

Madison Avenue: Buy Crest Toothpaste. Buy a Buick. Buy . . . Buy . . . Buy.

Your spouse: Honeeey, pleeeease take out the trash. Or, Honey, while you're up, may I have some coffee? And how about one of those ham sandwiches you do so well. Oh, and a few of your delicious cookies. . . .

The boss: Get it done NOW!

There are thousands of ways to persuade people to do what you want them to do. They range from mild flirtation to coercion.

Whether you are a salesperson or an engineer, here are some pointers to make yourself more persuasive.

- Be knowledgeable about your product or service. The hot air artists come a dime a dozen; don't be like them.
- Try not to argue. Arguing turns off people you want to impress. No one likes a know-it-all.
- When you're wrong, admit it. Disarm people before they have a chance to knock you.
- Show what's in it for the other guy. When people see dollar signs in your eyes, you've lost a sale. Be subtle and show how your product or service benefits them. Learn from salespeople who say, "Here's how my product can help you . . ."
- Be provocative. (Now you know why we have commercials.) Dare to be different; get their attention.
- Respect the other person. You don't have to befriend someone to make a sale; just show consideration.

NOBODY WINS AN ARGUMENT, BUT. . . .

A. L. Williams, the insurance and mutual fund magnate, doesn't believe in criticism. He believes that when you tell someone 99 positive things and 1 negative thing, that person tends to remember only the 1 negative thing.*

Williams isn't alone. Dale Carnegie (1888–1955) told us over 50 years ago, for the most part, not to criticize, complain, or condemn. Dale knew people often take criticism poorly. Still, criticism is sometimes necessary to solve or avoid problems at work. Without it, our country would be full of gladhanders and flatterers. So remember, criticism isn't the problem. It's the way you communicate it.

Here's how to voice criticism and complaints without offending others:

Don't Nuke Someone's Self-Esteem. When you criticize, do it with class. Keep things positive. Criticism is supposed to help, not wound.

"Talk in terms of behavior, not in terms of the person," says Dr. Harry Olsen, author of *The New Way to Compete*, (Lexington Books) and a leading human relations expert.

"Be careful of judgmental comments: You don't want to say, 'I can't believe how stupid you were to do that,' but rather, 'It looks like when you did . . . it didn't work out quite the way you wanted. Is there a way, perhaps, it could have worked out better? Now what can we do to make it easier the next time to . . . ?'" advises Dr. Olsen.[9]

Find Common Ground. Work to build understanding. Use remarks like, "I'm sure you can relate to this" or "I think you've seen this occur before" to break tension and keep things positive.

One Criticism at a Time. Keep your remarks brief and focused. You don't want to totally irritate or dishearten someone with too many gripes.

Be a Problem Solver. When you find fault, offer a possible solution. No one likes a whiner. By offering solutions, you show people you are working positively to improve the situation.

---

*A. L. Williams, *All You Can Do Is All You Can Do but All You Can Do Is Enough* (New York: Ivy Books, 1988), p.195.

Make a Call for Action. Diplomatically, specify what you would like to see happen as a result of your input. Then end the discussion on a friendly note.

DON'T BE A SCHLEMIEL

Maybe, just maybe, you rub people the wrong way. Good news: You don't have to be a clod for your entire life.

Dr. Hulsey Cason spent years studying behavior that tends to turn people off. Here's how it happens:

Are You Rubbing People the Wrong Way?
Do you:

Look depressed?	Tell dirty jokes at work?
Blow your stack?	Act disrespectful?
Chew gum like a cow?	Refer to co-workers as "honey,"
Act nosy?	"dude," or "babe"?
Argue habitually?	Have a gushing manner?
Hog the conversation?	Cut up to get attention?
Constantly criticize?	Brag about yourself?
Lie?	Use hard-sell tactics?
Cheat in games?	Act stuck-up?
Cut in line?	Smoke inconsiderately?
Give unasked-for	Talk too loud in public?
advice	Try to be funny?
Hurry others?	Overuse slang?
Coax others?	Make racist or sexist remarks?

Any of these aggravating habits sound familiar? If so, you need to make yourself a nicer person. Only when you stop rubbing people the wrong way can you hope to attract more friends, gain cooperation from co-workers, and reap more success at work.

PAY ATTENTION

You score points on style when you listen well. Listening well elevates the person who is talking; it relaxes him and makes him feel important.

The result? The person usually warms up to you and your ideas. Here are some ways to become a better listener:

Make the Other Person Think You're Interested. Even when you're tired, try to look like you're paying attention. Do this by nodding your head or leaning forward slightly during a conversation. It also helps to look the other person directly in the eye. (Resist the temptation to let your eyes wander.) And try not to glance at your watch, yawn, or cross your arms.

Clarify Main Points. Increase your understanding by summarizing main points. You can do this out loud or silently in your head. Repeat the main points by saying, ''Correct me if I'm wrong . . .'' or, ''That is one idea I've never heard before.''

Keep an Open Mind. Sometimes people act like Morris the cat, that finicky feline who achieved stardom in the popular Nine Lives cat food commercials of the 1970s and 1980s. He was fussbudgety about what he chose to eat.

Try not to be fussbudgety when you listen to people. Just because they have different viewpoints doesn't make them or their ideas any less important.

''There is no knowledge that is not power,'' said Ralph Waldo Emerson.* That's why you need to motivate yourself to listen actively. Always be on the lookout to pick up something from a conversation that gives additional insight and knowledge.

Listen to the Underlying Message. Pay attention to the underlying message of a conversation to better understand the other person. If someone tells you he hates sporting events, he might be trying to say he isn't athletic. If someone tells you all new cars are made poorly, she might be trying to say she can't afford a new car.

The New Lexicon Webster's Dictionary of the English Language (New York: Lexicon Publications, Inc., 1988), p. QD-73.

Put Yourself in the Other Person's Place. An empathic attitude can help you to listen more effectively. Ask yourself how you would feel if you had something important to say, but the person you were talking to looked uninterested.

Listen Critically and Analytically. Active evaluation helps you to analyze someone's ideas and increase your understanding. Conversations are often more enjoyable when you actively evaluate ideas instead of passively accepting them.

AT A GLANCE

Don't let a bad personality cost you money and success. Today, you need more than brains, talent, and hard work to get ahead; you also need to cultivate a winning personality.

Here's how you lead yourself to success:

Human Relations Strategies for the 90s

1. Make your boss work for you.
2. Make the first move.
3. Be sincere.
4. Greet your co-workers every day.
5. Offer a helping hand.
6. Don't be stingy with praise.
7. Make yourself persuasive.
8. Nobody wins an argument, but. . . .
9. Don't be a schlemiel.
10. Pay attention.

CHAPTER 3   AUTHOR INTERVIEWS

1. Elwood Chapman, May 31, 1990.
2. Thomas R. Horton, May 21, 1990.
3. Chapman, May 31, 1990.
4. Thomas L. Quick, May 15, 1990.
5. Ibid.
6. Veronica Booth, July 13, 1988.
7. Chapman, May 31, 1990.
8. Ty Ross, June 17, 1988.
9. Harry Olsen, August 11, 1989.

Chapter Four

Make the Butterflies in Your Stomach Fly in Formation

T his afternoon, without warning, your boss asks you to give a report at the monthly staff meeting.

You're scared, maybe terrified. Your knees begin to shake. Your heart beats faster. Your palms start sweating.

Worse yet, when you open your mouth—you babble.

Talk about a bad day at work! But take comfort; this classic dilemma is faced by millions of well-educated, talented people. When they have to speak in public, they're amateurs.

"To get ahead today, you need to communicate. And if you can't, you're just not going to be effective," says Dan G. S. Wright, a progressive branch manager with A. G. Edwards.[1]

Wright knows. He's seen legions of less-qualified employees steamroll over more deserving employees because they were better communicators.

OK, it's not fair. But who do you think a boss is going to promote—you, or someone who can:

- Sell potential clients on the firm.
- Give reports to civic, social, and religious clubs.
- Teach staff members new techniques.

- Speak on-the-spot in staff meetings.
- Manage problem clients and co-workers.
- Make a strong impression to get the account, make the sale, win the case, and so on.

This is the hard reality faced by millions of smart, hard-working people in their 20s, 30s, and 40s.

People who communicate well reap increased earnings, leadership opportunities, and, of course, job satisfaction. People who don't? Well, their careers often slow to a halt.

Don't let your lack of formal speech instruction get you down. In this two-part chapter, you learn both practical everyday speech skills *and* get a crash course in public speaking.

Enough said. Let's begin.

PART ONE: GOOD CONVERSATIONALISTS HAVE IT MADE

''You take two brilliant MBAs, one has a personality and the other doesn't; who wins?'' asks Dorothy Sarnoff, chairman of Speech Dynamics and coauthor of *Never Be Nervous Again* (Crown). ''The one with personality, of course.''[2]

You have to admit she has a point. Conversation skills are the key to building and promoting business and social relationships.

Still, people fumble with one-on-one communication. Introverts suffer silently, while hot-air artists come a dime a dozen. And there is no shortage of dull, stuffy people, either.

You owe it to yourself to improve your conversation skills. Whether you're at a staff meeting or a wedding reception, here are some techniques that can help you converse.

Secrets of Being a Good Conversationalist

1. Put the spotlight on the other person.
2. Phrase questions that spark conversation.
3. Show you know your stuff.
4. Be ready to speak on-the-spot.
5. Talk to brighten someone's day.

PUT THE SPOTLIGHT ON THE OTHER PERSON

"Perhaps the world's second worst crime is boredom. The first is being a bore."
Cecil Beaton

People, need I remind you, are hung up on their own problems, careers, and families. In fact, some self-absorbed people wouldn't listen at all if they didn't know they have to speak next.

Thirty-year-old Katherine learned this the hard way. "Last summer, I started dating Dan. He seemed nice, and I thought things were going well. But on our second date, he took me home at 9 P.M."

"Later I found out from a mutual friend that he thought I hogged the entire conversation. And you know something? He was right. Now, I try to be more attentive, and ask a question for each question I'm asked."

"You must make the other person the center of your conversation, or at least give them equal place in the conversation," says Dr. Marilyn Mathias Root, assistant professor of communication and assistant chairman of mass communications/public relations at Boston University.[3]

Show the other person you care; be attentive. This pays off in personal matters as well as business ones.

PHRASE QUESTIONS THAT SPARK CONVERSATION

What's wrong with this conversation?

JEFF
Is it hot outside?
BETH
Yes.
JEFF
Do you think the Chicago Bears will win their football game this weekend?
BETH
Yes.

Obviously, Jeff's conversation with Beth isn't working. She's not opening up.

Spencer Pugh, president of MAP Financial Group, knows how to get someone to open up. His secret? He asks questions that generate more than simple yes or no answers. Says Pugh:

> I use probing questions to stimulate conversation. If I want someone to open up, I ask questions that begin with how, what, where, when, and why. Someone can't answer yes or no to a question with those five leads.
>
> If I ask, "Are you happy?" "Did you go to Tampa last week?" "Do you like Sarasota?" someone can answer yes or no.
>
> For example:
> "Have you been to Miami?"
> "No."
> "Have you ever been to Chicago?"
> "No."
> "Have you ever been to New York?"
> "Yes."
> But if I ask, "How did you find New York?" someone can't say yes or no, she has to tell me.
>
> So, if I want someone to open up, I ask how, what, when, where, and why questions because the person has to talk. She may keep it short, but those questions open up the conversation, and that person will never open up if I ask questions that lead with: "Are you . . .?" "Did you . . .?" "Is . . .?"[4]

Let's look at a conversation that uses probing questions:

JEFF
Where are you going on vacation this year?
BETH
I'm going to Europe for two weeks in August.
JEFF
What countries will you be visiting this summer?
BETH
Spain, France, Germany, Switzerland, and, of course, England.
JEFF
Speaking of England, *what* do you think about the royal family?

Beth's answers tell Jeff more about herself. With, "Where are you going on vacation?" Beth could not answer yes or no—she was

STRATEGY

How to Talk to Practically Anyone

"The key to becoming a brilliant conversationalist is to act like a television interviewer," says Dorothy Sarnoff. "As long as you keep asking questions, people appreciate your company."[5]

Sarnoff also advises that you do your homework. This means keeping up with the latest news events, general interest topics, and developments in your profession. Read everything from *The Wall Street Journal* to *Time* magazine.

Now you need to gently prod people to talk about their favorite subject—themselves. The best way to do this is to ask questions that focus on job, family, and other interests.

Even if you're shy, here are questions that enable you to talk to practically anyone.

Spark Conversation with These 25 Questions

1. What do you do 9 to 5?
2. How long have you been . . . ?
3. What is a typical day like for a . . . ?
4. How do you like being a . . . ?
5. What do you like best about being a . . . ?
6. Where is your office?
7. Where are you from originally?
8. Tell me one thing about yourself that no one else knows.
9. What are your outside interests?
10. What do you like to do for fun?
11. What sports do you follow?
12. What movies have you seen lately?
13. What's your favorite television show?
14. How long have you . . . ? (Lived here, been married, worked there, etc.)
15. How large a family do you have?
16. How did you meet your husband (wife)?
17. What are you doing for . . . ? (New Year's Eve, Valentine's Day, and so on).
18. What do you think about . . . ? (Current event.)
19. What did you think of the meeting?
20. Where are you going on vacation this year?
21. Have you done your . . . (Christmas shopping, tax return, etc.) yet?
22. What are your plans for the weekend?
23. How was your weekend?
24. What's new and exciting in your life?
25. Where did you go to school?

forced to say that she was going to Europe. And when Jeff asked, "What countries will you be visiting?" she had to be specific.

Use probing questions; they generate more conversation.

SHOW YOU KNOW YOUR STUFF

"In terms of getting through the world, being able to speak on your feet is one of the most important skills that a person can have," says Kevin Dailey, president of Communispond, Inc.[7]

Consider this conversation at a commercial lending staff meeting:

BOSS
John, what do you think interest rates will be next June?
JOHN
Umm. I'm not sure, but I think they will level off. Uh . . . No, I mean they'll be going up.
BOSS
Susan, what direction do you think interest rates are headed?
SUSAN
I read an article in today's *Wall Street Journal* that suggests interest rates will probably remain stable because the consumer and producer price indexes did not fluctuate significantly from the previous month.

TIP

Don't Try Too Hard

In Chapter 3, you learned empathic listening skills. Those skills help you pick up on subjects that might interest the other person. But don't listen too hard, either. You might come off looking insincere.

"People often focus too much on trying to be good conversationalists," says Lewis Freeman, director of the speech program of Columbia University. Unfortunately, "Other people can tell if they're not paying a lot of attention to the conversation."[6]

Make someone feel important; listen and react to what they have to say. (Need a listening refresher? See Chapter 3.)

Fact: Bosses, clients, and co-workers often judge you professionally by your communication skills. Since Susan was able to answer competently, it's reasonable to assume she is equally as competent in performing her job.

Unfortunately, you don't have the luxury of time in today's business world. You must be able to speak on-the-spot.

BE READY TO SPEAK ON–THE–SPOT

"When someone asks me to say a few words about a project I'm working on, I get nervous," says Wanda, 24, an internal auditor. "With advance warning, I do fine, but the minute my supervisor wants instant answers at a staff meeting, I freeze."

There's no need to get tongue-tied. Whether it's introducing yourself at a meeting or defending yourself in a personnel review, just use the following plan to express your thoughts:

When Speaking On-the-Spot, Make Oral Paragraphs

1. Phrase your topic sentence. If you need to buy more time, restate the question you were asked.
2. Plan your answer. Make sure you have a definite introduction, body, and conclusion.
3. Support your topic sentence with more sentences (or ideas).
4. Summarize your answer.

Now let's map an example. What if your boss asks, "Should we buy an X or a Y computer system?"

Steps 1 and 2. Phrase both your introduction and topic sentence:

I like the X model better than the Y model.

Steps 2 and 3. Create a body of supporting sentences:

The X machine is more efficient because more than one employee can use it at the same time.

But the Y system doesn't have multiuser capabilities.

X offers better service, and if we have questions they offer reliable telephone support.

Step 4.   Summarize your answer:

For those reasons, I think we should buy the X system.

TALK TO BRIGHTEN SOMEONE'S DAY

An important part of conversation is knowing what subjects *not* to talk about. Consider avoiding the following topics.

Controversial Subjects.   Bosses and co-workers may like hot Buffalo chicken wings, but they don't like hot conversations.

Try to keep your conversation mild or medium. Avoid discussing controversial political and religious subjects with bosses and co-workers.

When your opinion is not in sync with others, it often works against you. People who don't share your contrary opinions may view them as a flaw in your character.

TIP

People associate excellent presentations and informed answers as evidence of professional ability. In other words, if you give a great speech, people may use it as evidence that you're also a good banker, lawyer, or salesperson.

Anything Depressing. Steer clear of mood deflating, depressing topics. Conversations about bank failures, incurable diseases, and serial killers make many people feel, well, anxious.

Locker Room Talk. Swear words may have been protocol in a college dorm, but not in the business world. If you routinely use bad language, bosses and co-workers may naturally assume that you lack class.

Subjects that Are Too Personal. It's also a good idea to avoid subjects that hit too close to home. Even if you are dying of curiosity about someone's serious health or personal problems, remember:

- If someone has been unemployed for a long time, don't ask, "Have you found a job yet?" He will be the first to tell you when he finds one.
- Don't ask for details if a co-worker's child is put in a drug rehabilitation program.
- Don't ask co-workers about the results of a biopsy. If they want you to know, they'll tell you.

There is a big difference between showing genuine concern and being nosy. Nosy people callously invade someone's personal space and provoke bad feelings.

PART TWO: COMPETENT SPEAKERS HAVE IT ALL

A senior vice president of a big company was conducting a meeting for 120 international managers in Miami.

The vice president stood up in front of the group at 9 A.M. and said, "Good morning, ladies and gentlemen." He paused. Then he said again, "Good morning, ladies and gentlemen." And paused. And then he said, "Good morning, ladies and gentlemen, I can't go on."

He stepped down and walked down the whole length of the room and out the door.

For many people, there is nothing tougher than speaking in public. They don't get much help in college because unfortunately, many large universities, even a prestigious Ivy League university such as Harvard, do not require students to take a public speaking course.

"When I was at State University of New York at Buffalo, public speaking was perceived by most students to be a basket-weaving course, not a challenging course," says Stuart J. Siegel, an associate manager for Jesup, Josephthal and Company, a NYSE member firm. "After graduation, we were in for a rude awakening."[8]

Employers often complain that both managers and entry-level employees lack basic communication skills. And listen to this: "Three thousand Americans were surveyed in a nationally projectable sample for their biggest fear," says Kevin Dailey. "Fear of public speaking was the number one fear stated by those respondents (even more than death). Nearly 41 percent of those respondents said that is what they feared most."[9]

Why do people fear public speaking? Dailey says, "Public speaking is fearful because suddenly we are totally exposed. When we are speaking, we are saying to other people, 'Be quiet. I'm going to make your time worthwhile, exciting, interesting, and stimulating. I'm going to reward you for your attention.'

"That puts a lot of pressure on us because we feel the audience, obviously a superior force, is sitting in judgment to see if we fulfil this implied promise. That can be very intimidating," says Dailey.[10]

OK, so you know public speaking is important, and you might not have had a lot of training. In this part of the chapter, you'll learn how to give effective speeches and seminars, control nervousness, and triumph over America's number one fear.

Luckily, it's really not that hard—it just takes a lot of practice. Here's the game plan:

The Rules of Public Speaking

1. Make the butterflies in your stomach fly in formation.
2. Concentrate on one message.
3. Be conversational.
4. Remember the do's and don'ts of public speaking.
5. Take a good speech course.

MAKE THE BUTTERFLIES IN YOUR STOMACH
FLY IN FORMATION

Never forget the audience when you plan a speech. They are VIPs. And remember that to be a successful speaker, you need to determine what your final goal is when you plan a speech.

"Good speakers analyze the audience with as much detail as possible," says Lewis Freeman of Columbia University. "Then they tailor the content, the structure, and the presentation of that speech to that group."[11]

There are three main types of prepared speeches:

1. If your goal is to educate or train, your purpose is to inform.
2. If you wish to speak for an audience's enjoyment or amusement, the purpose is to entertain.
3. Should you wish to influence or alter beliefs, the objective of your speech is to persuade.

Speech Objectives

Type of Speech	Example
Informative speech	Instruct a group of employees about changes in their health insurance coverage.
Entertaining speech	Share humorous stories about what it's like to be a member of the Jaycees.
Persuasive speech	Motivate a department to contribute their fair share to the United Way.

Once you select your topic and purpose, start planning your presentation. Get enough supporting material to clarify your ideas and subject matter. Support those ideas with examples, facts, statistics, descriptions, and visual aids.

Organize Your Material. Once you complete your research, start organizing your material into an outline. A good outline converts a hodgepodge of information into a well-organized speech

*On second thought, maybe I should have
taken a public speaking course in college.*

(one with a definite introduction, body, and conclusion) that helps
an audience follow your ideas.

"A good speaker knows where he's going and knows how to get
there in a talk," says Kevin Dailey.[12] Your *introduction* should pre-
view what you want your speech to accomplish. An attention-
grabbing device can help you induce an audience to listen. Questions, facts, statistics, quotes, stories, and opinions are some ways
to arouse interest.

The *body* of a speech makes the topic clear and understandable.
Use the right blend of descriptions, comparisons, and statistics to
help an audience understand your subject. And use visual aids: vi-
deotapes, films, slides, and flip charts.

Wrap up your speech with a good *conclusion*. It's an important
part of your speech because it's the last thing an audience remembers. A conclusion could be a summary of main ideas, a call for
action, or maybe a funny story.

Controlling Nervousness.   OK, your speech is constructed. Now what? Start rehearsing. "Preparation makes for confidence," says Dorothy Sarnoff. "It's a foolproof way to control nervousness."[13]

Sarnoff also advises practicing your speech at least four times. "If you will be standing when you give your speech, stand when you practice. Since you will be speaking aloud, practice aloud, not silent. Then practice one more time shortly before your presentation."[14]

Now relax. You'll do great.

CONCENTRATE ON ONE MESSAGE

"It is estimated that we only comprehend about 25 percent of any message we hear," says Dr. Marilyn Mathias Root. "So later retention might be as low as 10 percent."[15]

Don't worry if you forget to cover a point or two. Your audience probably won't have a clue. After two minutes, many members are probably adrift in their own problems. (God, how am I going to pay my VISA bill?)

Chances are, one month after your speech, your audience probably won't remember (or care) if you said, "Illinois gave $28.6 million in training funds to private industry last year." (Or should that have been $26.8 million?)

So what does that mean for you? You need to focus on the few things they *will* remember. First, focus on your speech's main message. If you're lucky, the audience will remember it.

Second, focus on your professional image. Subtly leave an audience with the impression that you're no amateur. Fortunately, this is not hard to do. Just show that you're confident, sincere, and knowledgeable during your presentation.

Remember:

- Build a speech with one main message you want to get across. Sell the theme; don't sweat the details.

- Audiences eventually remember less than 10 percent of what you said after a presentation.
- Many people have about a two-minute attention span.
- Leave the audience with a favorable glimpse of yourself.

BE CONVERSATIONAL

When you talk to an audience, be conversational; offer a glimpse of yourself. If you can, choose your words as you go along.

Watch note cards; they often act as a barrier between you and your audience. An audience is more receptive when they sense that your words come from your heart rather than from a 3 by 5-inch index card.

But what if you can't speak without notes? Try to speak from a one-page outline or use note cards sparingly. Break your speech down into divisible topics. After your introduction, talk about each subtopic for a minute or two, just like you would in a conversation.

Robert Orben, a famous speech writer and author, once said that "most speakers feel that 50 percent is what you deliver and 50 percent how you deliver it. Masters and Johnson feel the same way." (William Masters and Virginia Johnson conducted extensive research in the field of human sexuality and wrote the *Human Sexuality Report* in 1966.)

REMEMBER THE DO'S AND DON'TS OF PUBLIC SPEAKING

First, the Do's

- Make sure the audience knows why your speech benefits them.
- Encourage audience participation.
- Get your main message across.

Style versus Substance: Is It What You Say or How You Say It?

I asked three leading speech authorities, ''To be a successful speaker, should you emphasize what you say or how you say it?

Here's how they answered.

Dorothy Sarnoff, chairman of Speech Dynamics, answered: ''Did you know that 92 percent of an audience does not pay attention to the contents of a speech? Surveys show only 8 percent of the audience listens to content, 42 percent focuses on appearance and 50 percent on how the person speaks.''

''Still, substance is important, too. Even if your audience remembers less than 10 percent of what you said, they can still take notes.''[16]

Lewis Freeman, director of the speech program of Columbia University, answered:

''You can say all sorts of things wonderfully, and if the audience doesn't understand or if they leave not remembering what you say, it was useless.''[17]

Kevin Dailey, president of Communispond, Inc., answered: ''You always have to sell the fact that you're confident. Confidence comes partly through what it is you're saying and then significantly through how you say it. If your message is not something you *feel* confident about, it's rather difficult to *look* terribly confident.''[18]

- Keep your talk less than 20 minutes.
- Begin with a catchy introduction and end with a definite conclusion.
- Use humorous stories, jokes, and personal experiences—if they are appropriate.
- Anticipate questions that might be asked in the question-and-answer segment.
- Show the audience you're sincere and credible.
- Make a nice appearance.
- Show enthusiasm.
- Use hand and body gestures.
- Keep your eyes up; use natural eye contact.
- Project your voice.

TIP

Don't Memorize a Speech

Don't memorize speeches, unless your subject is so important that it might be misconstrued. (for example, a presidential address) You can look like you're on autopilot if your delivery sounds flat and mechanical. And you risk groping for your next sentence if you lose your train of thought.

- Vary the pitch and volume of your voice.
- Watch your speech on video.

Now the don'ts

- Say "ah," "uh," or use long audible pauses.
- Speak in a dull, monotone voice.
- Speak longer than the seat can endure.
- Get hung up on facts and statistics.
- Put your hands in your pockets, play with your eyeglasses, or fidget with your hair while you talk.
- Speak longer than your time allotment.

TAKE A GOOD SPEECH COURSE

I'm often asked to recommend a good public speaking course. After all, there are many speech courses out there.

Beware. Many courses have serious drawbacks: Some courses cost more than a thousand dollars, and you don't always get what you pay for. Other courses offer few opportunities to speak. (You need at least 10 to 15 such practical experiences.) And I can think of one popular course that offers practically no constructive criticism.

I'm a big believer in the Toastmasters program. It can really change you life. How do I know this? Well, it changed mine.

STRATEGY

Toastmasters Isn't a Wine-Tasting Club—

—But it is an international organization that can help you develop essential public speaking, reasoning, and listening skills. Toastmasters provides you the opportunity to improve by giving you the opportunity to speak regularly and receive constructive evaluation.

"There are more than 7,000 Toastmasters clubs and 160,000 members in the world," says John F. Noonan, international president of Toastmasters International.[19]

Many communities have a Toastmasters club that you can join for a nominal fee. Exxon Corporation, GE (General Electric Company), Xerox Corporation, and Eastman Kodak Company believe in the Toastmasters program so strongly that they sponsor their own company clubs.

"You will never lose the butterflies in your stomach," says Noonan. "But what Toastmasters training will do is to allow those butterflies to fly in formation."[20]

If I Went to a Meeting, What Would It Be Like?

Toastmasters uses a "learn-by-doing" format. Meetings resemble a stage play where members alternate functions each week.

So what's a meeting like?

The meeting begins. A toastmaster—the master of ceremonies—welcomes club members and guests to the meeting. He then introduces speakers and other members who have assigned functions.

Another club member then gives a brief invocation and pledge. Next, the week's laugh master tells a few jokes or humorous stories to relax the audience.

Three segments comprise the rest of the meeting. Segment 1 is table topics, an exercise where members speak on-the-spot. Segment 2 consists of prepared speeches. The final segment is evaluation.

During table topics, a table topics master asks five to seven members to speak impromptu. Table topics is an exercise where members speak on-the-spot without any advance preparation, for one to two minutes. Topics range from mandatory seat belts to "You're an animal in the zoo: What is your opinion on evolution?"

Next comes the prepared speech segment. Here, three or four members give formal speeches. Members learn to speak from a bare-bones outline or without notes.

No matter how advanced a speaker you are, Toastmasters speech manuals can improve your performance. Each manual has 5 to 10 speeches, with specific objectives, for you to customize and deliver to an audience. Before you can move on to the next speech, you must complete the objectives specified for the previous speech.

Beginning speakers concentrate on organization, vocal variety, and gestures. Advanced speakers choose speeches from *The Professional Salesperson*, *The Entertaining Speaker*, *Speeches by Management*, *Public Relations*, and other manuals.

Toastmasters is big on evaluation. Members always receive both positive and negative feedback.

During evaluation, the person assigned to critique a prepared speech tells what she liked or disliked. She then offers the speaker a few suggestions for constructive improvement; for example, "Stop smacking your lips."

Speakers also get a written evaluation from their evaluator. Critiques elaborate on points raised during oral evaluation and show how well speech objectives were met.

There are other evaluators who critique the whole meeting. A grammarian keeps track of incorrect grammatical usage. A timekeeper uses a stop watch and a timing light to help members stay within their time limit. And an "ah" counter drops a nail in a bucket or rings a bell each time someone says "ah," "uh," or uses an audible pause.

Toastmasters might be just what you need to become a better conversationalist, public speaker, and more effective leader.

AT A GLANCE

The connection between career advancement and strong communication skills is well documented. Work at improving your conversation and public speaking skills. They're essential to long-term career advancement.

Be a Better Conversationalist

1. Put the spotlight on the other person.
2. Phrase questions that spark conversation.
3. Show you know your stuff.
4. Be ready to speak on-the-spot.
5. Talk to brighten someone's day.

Be a Better Public Speaker

1. Make the butterflies in your stomach fly in formation.
2. Concentrate on one message.
3. Be conversational.
4. Remember the do's and don'ts of public speaking.
5. Take a good speech course.

CHAPTER 4   AUTHOR INTERVIEWS

1. Dan G. S. Wright, August 3, 1988.
2. Dorothy Sarnoff, May 7, 1990.
3. Marilyn Mathias Root, May 8, 1990.
4. Spencer Pugh, August 30, 1988.
5. Sarnoff, May 7, 1990.
6. Lewis Freeman, May 9, 1990.
7. Kevin Dailey, May 11, 1990.
8. Stuart J. Siegel, May 8, 1990.
9. Dailey, May 11, 1990.
10. Ibid.
11. Freeman, May 9, 1990.
12. Dailey, May 11, 1990.
13. Sarnoff, May 7, 1990.
14. Ibid.
15. Root, May 8, 1990.
16. Sarnoff, May 7, 1990.
17. Freeman, May 9, 1990.
18. Dailey, May 11, 1990.
19. John F. Noonan, May 14, 1990.
20. Ibid.

Chapter Five

Sometimes You Have to Go Against Instinct

To find out what is on the mind of today's white-collar worker, I interviewed more than 100 employees, at all levels, and I sent a career survey to men and women in selected Jaycees' chapters throughout the United States.

At the end of each interview, I asked each person, "What was your biggest career obstacle?" I could sense that old wounds were being reopened. Invariably, there was a long pause before the answers came.

The career survey asked the same question. Responses ranged from "getting past someone who slept with the boss" to "lack of management integrity."

Here are some of the big obstacles these people faced and strategies to handle them if they should happen to you:

Career Obstacles of the 1990s

1. You.
2. Illegal or unethical demands.
3. Mergers.
4. Making a big mistake at work.

5. Making more money.
6. Inadequate education or lack of specialized training.
7. Your boss breaks a major promise.
8. Difficult bosses and co-workers.

The next chapter, ''Breaking Through the Glass Ceiling,'' focuses on special career problems of women in corporate America.

YOU

''Not knowing what I wanted to do in my life.''

''Too many career changes.''

''Finding a job I can grow with.''

''Getting a job in my field.''

''Obtaining a job where I have a future.''

Only you can decide what is best for your career; if you don't take charge of your own career development, no one else will. A major step in overcoming some career obstacles is to acknowledge your contribution to them. Let's take a look at four big ones:

Getting Your Foot in the Door.   *Help Wanted* . . . Only people with *experience* need apply. Help Wanted, *Professional* . . . 3–7 years *experience* required.

Many companies no longer view employees as assets to train. Who can blame them? They've been burned too many times. After investing a fortune in training, new employees often change jobs at the first chance to earn another three grand a year.

Now these companies say, ''Let's hire experienced employees who can be productive immediately. They won't just take the training and experience we gave them and run.''

OK, companies want experience. But how can you get experience if companies don't hire you because you don't have experience? Talk about a catch-22!

When it comes to getting your first job, you don't have a lot of options. Be patient. It may take months to break into some professions. This is especially true if you limit your job search to a few cities.

But if you really want to break into some professions, you may have to move. You may have to take your first job where you can get it. This may mean working in Storm Lake, Iowa, even though your family lives in Atlanta, Georgia.

Know When to Change Jobs.   Stay at a company as long as you are learning, growing, and being recognized for your contributions. When that stops, it's time to change jobs.

There are times you must change jobs to achieve your career objectives. This is especially true if you aspire to a top-management job. Try to avoid lateral moves by accepting the same position at a different company.

Don't Limit Yourself.   "People apologize for why they never got to be vice president of finance, vice president of personnel, when opportunities abound," says Ronald C. Pilenzo, president of the Society for Human Resource Management.[1]

"But one, you've got to be ready. And two, you have to have competence and confidence in yourself. And three—you've got to seek opportunities—wherever they are!

"It's nice to say, 'You know, I'd like to stay in this town.' But if you limit yourself, choices won't be too great.

"Too many people apologize for where they are by rationalizing why they couldn't relocate, because their kids are going to school and are members of the soccer team," says Pilenzo.[2]

Of course, family concerns are valid reasons for not moving, but there may be some consequences to pay. You might not achieve all of your career goals. But, then again, you might be willing to sacrifice some career satisfaction for a more satisfying life. You make the call.

Make a Commitment. ''I think it is essential at some point in your career to make a major commitment,'' says Ross Webber, a professor of management at Wharton School at the University of Pennsylvania. ''Common wisdom is that somewhere between your late 20s and age 40 you had better demonstrate competence over a major period of time in a major sequence of jobs.''[3] (This means advancing through several positions at the same company for at least seven years.)

''I don't think movement before your 30s particularly hurts you,'' says Webber. ''But strive to find a career in an organization you like by your early 30s.''

''I think movement during your 30s, particularly age 36 or 37, definitely hurts you. And I think there is a period in there that you must demonstrate sustained achievement.'' This helps to put you

Sometimes you have to go against instinct to overcome many career obstacles. It may seem unnatural, but the results will be worth it.

in line for a major move either in the same position or someplace else in your late 30s or 40s.

"Your peak years for career progression, in terms of size of jump, is roughly 40 to 45. That is the critical promotion. If you're not poised by the early 40s, in terms of the top levels of your organization, you're not likely to get there," says Webber.[4]

Remember, try to commit to a career and an organization by your late 20s or early 30s. But don't lose heart if you've passed 30 and haven't found your niche. Just remember: Life is full of opportunities, but *you* have to be the one to see them.

ILLEGAL OR UNETHICAL DEMANDS

Here's a hypothetical situation:

> You're in a real bind. Today, your firm's managing partner gives you a sales agreement for a large strip-shopping center to record.
>
> He tells you, "I know it's wrong, but back date the document as if the property had been sold last year. The client doesn't want to pay a lot of extra taxes."
>
> Then, to make matters worse, he expects you to witness the client's signature at the signing!
>
> While the IRS probably won't find out about the altered document, you know it's considered fraud to back date an agreement.
>
> You need your job, at least for the time being; you're a single parent with two kids to support. What should you do?

Refuse to do anything illegal or immoral. Regardless of the circumstances, you should not put yourself on the line to do something illegal.

Instead, tell your boss, "Look, I'm not going to do it because it is going to hurt both of us," says David L. Bradford, a lecturer in organizational behavior at the Stanford Graduate School of Business. "Sooner or later, illegal acts get found out."[5]

Then turn an awkward situation into a positive one. Ask your boss, "Why do you want to do this? What is the goal?" After the boss tells you the reasons, say, "Let's find another way to do this."

But what if your boss says, "Well, if you don't do it, you won't get anywhere in this department, and I may fire you."

Ask yourself these questions: Do you have your facts straight? Can you hold your own in court? Are the "iffy" short-term rewards worth a tarnished reputation? Jail?

Speaking of court, you need to ask yourself the same question the prosecuting attorney is likely to ask later: "And when you observed this happening, what did you do?"

You want to be able to say, "I reported it to the personnel department in confidence." Because if you don't, the prosecutor is going to say, "Well, how is it you knew about this—and didn't report it?"

The short-term rewards of doing something illegal or unethical are usually *very* iffy. And the long-term consequences can blow up in your face when other managers or the authorities find out. "You're going to be in trouble," says Marilyn Moats Kennedy, president of Career Strategies.[4] "Not always legal trouble, but your reputation is going to be trashed."[6]

Now it's time to meet with personnel. Let them know your job is on the line because you *won't* do something illegal or immoral. Understand, though, that your boss may still fire you to cover his tracks.

But what if your company doesn't have a personnel department? Or, what if personnel takes your boss's part?

Save your hide: Keep all relevant documentation for future reference. Photocopy records. Make detailed notes of conversations. Record dates, times, and names. And start looking for a new job. You're probably better off changing jobs (even if the new job doesn't have group dental) than working for a crooked boss.

Some bosses still might not take no for an answer. When a boss tells you for the last time, "Do it or you're fired," just say, "Go ahead. I refuse to do anything illegal or immoral. I don't want to go to court, but I'm prepared to get a lawyer." You've got nothing to lose—many wrongful discharge suits exceed $100,000 in damages.

TIP

Work for an Ethical Company

Ethics come from the top. Large companies are now striving to improve ethics.

More and more companies are saying, "These are the ethical standards we believe in as an organization, and we expect our employees to adhere to them. And we will rigorously enforce those ethical standards. Employees who don't follow them will be punished."[7]

Unless the standards of ethics come *from the top*, you're going to have to do battle with sleazy reptiles who say, "I know it's wrong, but go ahead and do it, anyway."

MERGERS

Another situation:

You work for a large bank that is going through a merger. You're 48, and you're worried. Even though the new company sent a memo saying your job is safe, you don't believe them.

Their past track record with mergers isn't good. Usually they have a big management shake-up a few months after the merger. You're at an age where it's tough to find a new career position, especially one with the same money and benefits.

How should you react to the merger? Should you start sending out resumes? Or, should you try to weather the storm?

Here are some thoughts on coping with mergers:

Beware of Duplication.   Remember, companies need one payroll department, one marketing department, and so on. Mergers can cause duplication of these departments. Jobs in departments that don't duplicate services are usually safe; however, if you think your job is shaky because you work in a department that duplicates services, request a transfer to another department (or even start sending out some resumes).

Beware. You may get the option of a transfer, but then again you might not. You may work a few months and get a note that says, "Effective December 31, your department will stop operation."

Watch Your Attitude.   Usually a few months after a merger the incoming company assesses employees for skill, ability, and attitude.

Attitude is the big test. You don't want to force their hand by viewing the merger negatively.

"Often you can tell who is going to survive a merger and who is going to get cut," says R. Wayne Smith, a branch manager with Barnett Bank. "Those who are enthusiastic and show cooperation with the company usually make it. But those who hinder, second guess, or bad-mouth get the pink slips."[8]

Here are tips to come out on top of a merger.

- Don't poison the morale of other employees.
- Don't sit around in a depressed mood, waiting for the ax to fall.
- Don't publicly mourn the loss of your old company by making remarks like, "We used to do it this way." Get real! The new company doesn't care how you used to do something. Do it the way they tell you to do it.
- Act fully cooperative.
- Act enthusiastic.
- Make an effort to meet the new management team.
- Learn all new procedures.

Age.   Age plays a big part in the merger. If you're single and 28, you can usually find a new job more easily than someone who is 48 and has kids in college.

Someone who is well vested in a pension plan has much more to lose than a young person. If you're single, you're less likely to have a mortgage and you can move to another state for another job more easily than someone with a spouse and children.

TIP

Don't Start a Business in Your 50s

You may get a big lump-sum pension distribution when you lose your job. And when you see all that money, it's tempting to start your own business. You know how it is in America—everybody wants to own his or her own restaurant.

But statistics show most new small businesses fail. Don't let your dream of owning your own business become a nightmare. If your business bombs, your senior years won't be golden. Remember, your pension distribution may be your only real financial security.

For example, if I were 48, I'd want to know "What type of pension benefits do I have? Does this organization have a severance pay plan?" In other words, find out your financial position. This way, you're economically prepared if somebody says, "We are having a cutback because we just merged. I'm sorry, but we're going to have to let you go."

Seniority Is No Defense.   Dependable but average employees often lose in mergers. The new team has to have a reason to keep them on the payroll, and working for the company for a long time usually is not reason enough.

Whether you've been at a company six weeks or 20 years, you must prove yourself all over again. The new company puts everything that is in the past—in the past.

When to Crank Out Your Resume.   When it comes to mergers, it never hurts to send out a few resumes. Don't let it affect your attitude, though. You still have to focus on doing a good job for the acquiring company; you may decide to stay, after all.

Jump If Necessary, but Don't Jump Prematurely.   "Sometimes people jump prematurely," says Pilenzo. "Some cases where mergers have taken place, some people have come out for the better, and they've been promoted. Sometimes the management gets terminated and the rest of the people are promoted into better and higher level positions."[9]

Cushion the Fall.   Sit down with your boss or personnel department and negotiate a tough severance pay package. Most people think if the severance plan says, "You have *x* years, so you get *y* numbers of weeks in severance pay."

"If I sat down and they tried to give me four weeks pay, I'd try to get eight weeks pay," says Pilenzo. "If I couldn't get that, I'd try to get them to extend my hospital coverage for the next year, or have them hire an outplacement consultant."[10]

MAKING A BIG MISTAKE AT WORK

It happens when you least expect it. Then it comes back to haunt you. You catch it before the boss does. Let's explore what to do when you make a monumental blunder at work. Marilyn Moats Kennedy has some suggestions.[11]

What Do You Do When You Make a Mistake at Work?

Question: What should an employee do if he makes a mistake at work?
Kennedy: I would go to the person in charge and say, "I made a mistake on this project. This is what I've done to remedy it. How does that sound to you?" I certainly wouldn't wait for it to be discovered; that would be horrible.
Question: Is it ever appropriate for an employee to cover his tracks?
Kennedy: No. Figure it out. Fix it, and then tell.
Question: Should an employee ever fix it and not tell?
Kennedy: What if it's discovered? Someone is going to say, "Why didn't you tell me that?" And it is also going to depend on the kind of boss you have. Most bosses don't want to be surprised. This way, you don't surprise them.

When you make a mistake at work, take Kennedy's advice: Fix it, and then tell.

MAKING MORE MONEY

"Income!"

"$"

"Pay raises!"

"The rating system for promotions and raises."

Want to score more money? Just logically show your boss you're worth it. Base your request on performance—not tenure or seniority.

"A lot of people make the mistake of walking in and asking for money that has nothing to do with the work, like 'I have a son go-

---

TIP

How to Get Bigger Salary Increases

- Ask for interim minireviews to see how you are doing; improve performance before your annual review.
- Keep a work journal that documents job accomplishments.
- Don't wait for performance appraisal time to lobby for money. Campaign for money when budgets are being set.
- Beware: If a department head can allocate a 5 percent increase for salaries, one employee might get zero and another employee might get 10 percent.
- Don't threaten to quit if you don't get a raise.
- Strike when you're red hot. If you do something extraordinary at work (land a major contract, develop a plan that saves the company big money), ask for a raise.
- If you have a poor review with no salary increase, ask your boss for another salary review in two months if your performance improves.
- Take the initiative; ask for the raise.
- Make sure your boss notices your hard work. (See Chapter 2).
- Show that the quantity and quality of your work is high.
- Ask for more money than you expect. If you want a 7 percent raise, ask for 10 percent.

ing to college.' Who cares? Or 'I have to buy a new car.' Who cares?'' says Thomas Quick, executive director of Resource Strategies Institute.[12]

Take time beforehand to write a list of your job accomplishments. Write down at least six significant accomplishments over the past year. Emphasize results: Show your contribution to major projects.

''Many times, bosses need this, too,'' says Dan Murphy, president of Corporate Dynamics. ''It's very easy for a boss to take a good worker for granted, and that is why it is always good for the employee to realize that you've got to go in there and sell that boss why you need a raise. And have it down what you've accomplished.''[13]

Now you're armed. Schedule a meeting with the boss. Let your list set the agenda. ''Show how you return more to the company than they are paying you,'' says Kennedy. ''Stress your role in achieving company objectives and resolving company problems.''[14]

As you move down the list, observe how your boss is reacting. Now request your salary increase. If your boss agrees with your list, you'll get your increase.

INADEQUATE EDUCATION OR LACK OF SPECIALIZED TRAINING

''Not finding my niche and the amount of money I desire.''

''Being qualified for a job but being overlooked because of not having a college degree.''

''Not having an MBA.''

''Undergraduate degree is not from a 'name school.' The Ivy League is endorsed very heavily at my current employer.''

You work hard. Damn hard. You're good at your job, too. But your career is stalled. No matter what you do, you just can't overcome not having an undergraduate degree, a graduate degree, or some special training.

TIP

Many government jobs allow equivalent work experience to count for a college degree.

All things being equal, many employers choose to promote a degreed candidate over a nondegreed candidate.

Why all the emphasis on a piece of sheepskin? Employers view degrees as evidence of being able to achieve goals. In other words, if you overcome obstacles to get a BS degree, you'll likely work just as hard to overcome obstacles on tough projects. Their logic isn't flawless, but that's the way it is.

Here's how you can make it without the "right" credentials:

Change Jobs.   "Not having a college degree hasn't hurt me at Coast Federal," says Lynn Barnett, a branch manager with Coast Federal Savings and Loan Association.[15] Lynn was promoted by president Robert Antrim, who doesn't have a four-year college degree, either.

Work for a company that respects experience and ability. You may get more opportunities in a company where many bosses and owners don't have college degrees. They probably won't hold something against you that they don't have themselves.

Go Back to School.   "In my office, a bachelor's degree is a dime a dozen," says Mark Sorrels, a manager with American Airlines. "It's almost like a high school diploma. But to excel and get ahead of the next guy . . . I'm going back for my MBA."[16]

Take it from Mark. If it means going to night school, go to night school. If it means taking a leave of absence, take a leave of absence. Do whatever it takes. Just get the education and training you need.

Most public schools, community colleges, and universities offer courses at night or on weekends that make you more promotable. There are also a lot of good home-study programs.

Be Tenacious.   You may be able to advance in your present company even without the right credentials. Start by volunteering for jobs. Build clout for yourself by doing those jobs well.

Now take the initiative; ask for more responsibilities. Make sure you do high-quality work. Then ask your boss if you can participate in training programs. If she says no, keep trying until she gives you your big break.

Don't let your lack of education get you down. Search for an opportunity in a company that appreciates you or bite the bullet and go back to school.

YOUR BOSS BREAKS A MAJOR PROMISE

"My first job after college was as an account executive with a major NYSE brokerage firm," says Paul, 33. "My career progressed nicely. So nicely that five years out of school I was earning in the low six figures."

"One day, John, a district manager for another firm, asked me to lunch. He had an opening in his firm's Orlando office. John promised that if I came on board, he would promote me to branch manager in three months—now that was an opportunity.

"To make a long story short, I gave notice.

"The first few months went well. I opened many new accounts, and everyone said I was doing a good job. Right on schedule, John fired the Orlando office manager.

"Later, I saw John at a conference and he said, 'I haven't forgotten about you, Paul.' Naturally, I thought he was about to make good on his promise to make me branch manager.

"Two weeks went by. Then I got this jolt:

MEMO: Distribute A to Z.

It gives me great pleasure to announce that Walter B. will be the new branch manager . . .

"Is it too late to make good on John's promise? What should I say to John?"

TIP

Help a Boss Remember a Major Promise

Get significant details of *major* promises in writing when you accept new employment. "Specify responsibilities and obligations on both sides, so that there are no misunderstandings down the road," says Dan Murphy.[18]

While you can't always enforce them legally, they're still tangible evidence. A boss can't defend himself by saying, "No, you misunderstood me."

Play it safe. Remind bosses of their major promises: "Now, John, when will I move into the manager's office?" is a subtle way of doing this. Don't be a pest, though.

More than anything, if you smell a rat, confront the issue immediately. You may have time to resolve a matter in your favor, but once the deed is done—you're powerless.

Confront John. Find out exactly what his reasons were for promoting Walter, and—they had better be good. Now look at the facts. If you missed the promotion because you're getting a better position—fine.

But what if John doesn't have a good reason?

"See if there are other opportunities in the same organization," says Ross Webber. "Can you make contact with other managers that might have opportunities? If those possibilities aren't workable, make plans to leave."[17]

Take heed: Sometimes you lose to an unscrupulous boss.

DIFFICULT BOSSES AND CO-WORKERS

"Working for an insecure boss."

"Personalities."

"My boss being a basic bastard—not realizing people are human!"

"Other employees and co-workers."

"Jealous co-workers."

Another situation:

> I work with Cheryl. In a word, she's . . . difficult.
>
> When I make a mistake at work, no matter how small, she immediately tells my manager. But when I catch her mistakes, which is often, I correct them or ask her to make a few changes.
>
> She also bad-mouths me to other co-workers. She makes remarks like, "I can't believe how cocky he is," or "He's not going to last long around here."
>
> Nothing I do helps me to get along with Cheryl. In fact, during my last performance review, I was castigated for not getting along with some of my co-workers (translation: Cheryl).
>
> What can I do to get along with Cheryl?

"If there is a problem with a co-worker, you should go to the co-worker and say, 'We seem to have difficulties. Let's work it out,'" says Marilyn Moats Kennedy. "And if the person says, 'There is no difficulty,' don't retreat. You must move in closer and say, 'Well, good. If there's no difficulty, let's have lunch!'"[19]

"Sit down with a co-worker or boss and explain what is going on and how this is affecting you," says Dan Murphy. "Often, the other person might not be even aware of it. Attempt to communicate and see how the situation can be resolved. The worst thing to do is to hold in and suppress it and let it come out in other negative ways."[20]

Mark Sorrels, a manager with American Airlines, transferred jobs because his college degree and job knowledge intimidated his boss.

"If I had it to do over again, I would have gone back to my supervisor and let her know I was there to do a good job and learn from her," says Sorrels. "Then I'd ask her, 'Why can't we work together to come up with ideas instead of working against each other?'"[21]

When in trouble, let the other person know you just want to resolve your differences.

AT A GLANCE

To make it to that corner office, you need to clear some mighty big career obstacles. Here are some you're likely to encounter:

Career Obstacles of the 1990s

1. You.
2. Illegal or unethical demands.
3. Mergers.
4. Making a big mistake at work.
5. Making more money.
6. Inadequate education or lack of specialized training.
7. Your boss breaks a major promise.
8. Difficult bosses and co-workers.

CHAPTER 5 AUTHOR INTERVIEWS

1. Ronald C. Pilenzo, May 18, 1990.
2. Ibid.
3. Ross Webber, May 21, 1990.
4. Ibid.
5. David L. Bradford, May 21, 1990.
6. Marilyn Moats Kennedy, May 16, 1990.
7. Pilenzo, May 18, 1990.
8. R. Wayne Smith, June 1, 1988.
9. Pilenzo, May 18, 1990.
10. Ibid.
11. Kennedy, May 16, 1990.
12. Thomas L. Quick, May 15, 1990.
13. Dan Murphy, May 16, 1990.
14. Kennedy, May 16, 1990.
15. Lynn Barnett, August 31, 1988.
16. Mark Sorrels, January 12, 1989.
17. Webber, May 21, 1990.
18. Murphy, May 16, 1990.
19. Kennedy, May 16, 1990.
20. Murphy, May 16, 1990.
21. Sorrels, January 12, 1989.

Chapter Six

Breaking Through the Glass Ceiling

When the surveys started rolling in from all across the county, I received some surprising responses from women. Here are some actual answers to the question, ''What has been your greatest career obstacle?''

''Men!''

''Being female in management.''

''Misogynists'' (men who hate women).

''Overcoming prejudice against women.''

''Working in a conservative, male-dominated career where the senior managers still have old-fashioned ideas about women.''

''Men's attitudes regarding females.''

I asked Kate White, editor-in-chief of *Working Woman* magazine, about those responses. ''I think women baby boomers have all had some incorrect expectations,'' she told me.[1] ''Women who came out of college in the early 70s had incredibly high expectations and were surprised about some of the barriers they came up against.

"I'll make it to the top."

"Perhaps the next wave of the baby boomers thought, 'OK, some of those barriers have been broken down.' Only to discover, 'Oh, no—not as many as I thought!'" says White.

And women coming out of college today might think *all* the barriers are broken down—only to discover that there is still, even among their peers, discrimination.

"Discrimination is *still* tricky for women, but today it's more subtle and harder to put your finger on it," says White.

She also thinks women won't join upper management in significant numbers until a younger, different type of man replaces many top-level managers, now in their 50s and 60s, who will retire in the next 20 years. "A man whose wife works, who understands the problems and has worked with women himself can see having a woman in his inner circle," says White.[2]

Until that happens, and it will, use this chapter to help you:

1. Break through the glass ceiling into upper management.
2. Get noticed.

3. Build rapport with male bosses and co-workers.
4. Overcome special problems of women managers.
5. Confront sex and race discrimination.
6. Deal with sexual harassment.
7. Handle a spouse who resents your income.

First, let's look at some strategies that can help women (and men) break into middle and upper management.

BREAK THROUGH THE GLASS CEILING INTO UPPER MANAGEMENT

Women have long been divided about why so few women have made it into upper-management positions. Here are some of their opinions:

- Sexual discrimination.
- The men promoted were thought to be more qualified.
- Women often work in secretarial and clerical jobs.
- Family responsibilities limit time that can be devoted to a fast-track career.
- It is only since the early 1970s that women have entered business schools in significant numbers.

Getting into upper management if you're a woman is like being a quarterback in a football game without referees. It's a tough game and a lot of players play dirty.

Like any game, there are obstacles, and this one has a big one called the *glass ceiling*, an obstacle that allows women to see but prevents them from grabbing many top middle- and upper-management jobs.

Carolyn Elman, executive director of the American Business Women Association, believes that many women need to learn what it takes to break through a glass ceiling. "They need to know how to size up a company and figure out whether they can make it into upper management," she says.[3]

Assessing your chances of making it into upper management requires detective work, and much of this needs to be done before you accept a job. Start by looking at the organization's track record in moving women up the ladder.

"If a woman is going into an organization and there are no women at the top, she ought to be prepared to be a trailblazer or know that is not a place to be," says Constance Berry Newman, director of the Office of Personnel Management in Washington D.C., where she's responsible for more than 2.2 million federal employees.[4]

"You need to look at the environment to which you're moving, and if the environment is one that has not produced other women in the past, the chances are the myth is backed up by fact. And that may not be the place for you unless you're willing for other reasons to go into the organization and get good experience and—possibly break the glass ceiling—but maybe not," she adds.

Once you're on the payroll, however, it's a different story. You need to determine what the company expects and rewards. "If there are women up the line, talk with them, and talk with some of the top men in the organization," says Newman. "Find out what steps you need to take to move up the ladder." And let it be known you expect to go up in the company and will back up your goal with superior performance.

While a good game plan is essential, you also need to convince superiors you expect to advance as steadily as male rivals. Start by openly expressing interest in jobs one level above your current job, discuss prerequisites, and drop hints about timetables.

But once you realize that your opportunities for advancement are exhausted (or worse, for some reason never existed), consider changing jobs. "I think that unless you are trying to be a crusader, there is no need to hang around someplace and try to change everybody when you're not going to be able to do it," says Newman.[5]

Carolyn Elman agrees. "Men do it all the time. I think women need to quit hitting their heads against the wall and look at what upper management is like, and if it looks like they won't join the club—figure out a strategy to break in or find a company where they fit in," says Elman.[6]

Let's run down some more suggestions to break through a glass ceiling:

Have an Approachable Manner. Don't sabotage your career with lousy interpersonal skills. "Most people are successful in jobs because of how they deal with other people and how they work in teams," says Constance Berry Newman.[7]

Newman also believes women should work extra hard at improving interpersonal and team-building skills. "When I hire, I don't only look at an individual and individual scores. But I think about everybody else I have in the organization, and how these people are going to relate to get the job done—and that is very subtle, making that call."

Tip: Make an effort to be friendly, cooperative, and personable with all superiors and co-workers, not just those with clout.

Make Personal Sacrifices. Some experts believe that if a woman really aspires to upper management, she's going to have to make a lot of sacrifices—especially in terms of her personal life.

"One of the great myths of business is only the women make the sacrifices," says Jo Foxworth, president of Jo Foxworth, Inc., and author of *Wising Up* (Dell) and *Boss Lady* (Crowell). "This is not true. Men sacrifice a very great deal for their careers.

"There are so many men who haven't had a vacation with their families—ever. And others who rarely have an uninterrupted weekend with them, or even an uninterrupted evening. . . . I think they should be prepared to make all the sacrifices for their careers that men make," says Foxworth.[8]

Don't Be a Trailblazer Unless You Want to. Any company that is dominated by men is less likely, at least statistically, to promote you into upper management. Or it will likely promote you at a slower rate than at a company where women already hold top management positions.

But what am I telling you that for? You already know the odds. So why not consider a job in a company where you don't have to constantly fight uphill battles (unless you want to)? Industries such as publishing, retailing, and cosmetics can be gold mines of opportunity because many women already hold positions of power.

Beware of Mentors. ''I think women should spend less time looking for women mentors because that is putting responsibility on another person for one's career,'' says Constance Berry Newman.[9]

Don't pin all your hopes for advancement on a mentor; you can look ridiculous if your mentor gets fired or demoted. Or worse yet, upper management may view you as your mentor's protege or lapdog, not someone who is independent. Still, if you find a mentor who gives you a break or two, go for it.

Security Can Work against Upper-Management Aspirations. Recognize that the security of group health insurance and other benefit plans such as a 401K plan may keep you from pursuing a lucrative and satisfying career position at another company. In fact, some people hesitate to change jobs because they fear even a few well-timed job changes will look bad on their resumes.

Wrong! As long as they move shrewdly from one good job to a better job, one with more responsibility, they probably won't get pegged as compulsive job changers. (A compulsive job changer is someone who routinely changes jobs without gaining significant titles or skills.)

Benefit packages are enticing, and you need them, but you may have to change jobs to score an upper-management position. (Note: This strategy works better for women below age 32. And it often works for other women who feel their prospects for making it into upper management, at their present companies, are slim or nonexistent if they're willing to risk secure jobs in order to achieve major career goals.)

Goals. Start by setting your ultimate career goal. Then design short-range and intermediate goals to help you reach that goal. Put your plan in writing and make sure you develop a definite timetable. Now you're ready to act. Remember to constantly monitor and evaluate your progress.

Line Jobs Are Still the Most Direct Way to the Top.   Steer clear
of dead-end jobs. Line jobs usually offer more long-term opportunities than staff jobs like public relations and personnel. If you
want a six-figure income and a top management job, consider
avoiding some staff jobs that can't advance past middle rungs of
the company ladder.

No Guts, No Glory.   Seek out risky projects that are immediately apparent on your company's bottom line. If you participate in
projects that make a lot of extra money for the company, you are
bound to be rewarded with a higher ranking executive job.

Show Gritty Self-Determination.   Walk away from self-doubt
forever. There are times in a career that you just don't take no for
an answer. Focus on being a problem solver. When you really believe in a project and hit snags, always look at alternatives that
make a project workable. Persistence and industriousness are essential if you want a fast-track career.

Work for a Smart Company.   Women made up 43 percent of the
total work force in 1980. By the year 2000, they will account for
more than 47 percent of the total work force, and more than 60 percent of all women will be employed. Smart companies are already
responding to those changing demographics; they're training and
developing more women, and promoting them to important top-
management positions.

Be an Entrepreneur.   "If the world doesn't change by the time
my infant daughter turns age 24, I would encourage her to be an
entrepreneur, and not go through all the corporate lip-service,"
says *Working Woman*'s Kate White. "I would encourage her to start
her own business and do something brilliant. For so many women
it has been very frustrating, and they haven't reached the benefits.
If things don't change, I would never encourage my daughter to go
that route."

Instead, "I'd say, Get a brilliant idea. Package it. Maybe work in
a company for a couple years and make some contacts. Learn the

---

What Men Get Wrong about Women in Corporate America

Question: What do you think most male managers get wrong about women employees? Let's hear what the panel had to say:

Alma Baron, professor emeritus at the management Institute School of Business at the University of Wisconsin:

> "I think male managers will take one woman and extrapolate to all women," says Baron. "Let's say if Ed screws up, they say, 'Well, there is poor Ed and he screwed up.' But if Elaine screws up, they say, 'Well, you can't trust a woman.'
>
> I think if one woman promises to come back after a pregnancy and doesn't show up, they often take the view that *all women* will not come back after pregnancy. Whereas if one man makes an error, they say, Let's get rid of *him* because he was untrustworthy to begin with."[11]

Kate White, editor-in-chief of *Working Woman* Magazine:

> It's easy to misinterpret working women who are married and have kids, and want to be home for those kids, as not giving their all to the job.[12]

Constance Berry Newman, director of the Office of Personnel Management:

> Many male managers think a woman is not as tough as a man. . . . They make certain assumptions because women have different styles of leadership and their voices aren't as strong. But I think they are as wrong as they can be when they think the woman aren't as tough as they are. They might even be tougher.[13]

---

ropes. Get an MBA. And then do it on your own, baby—and make a billion dollars!' " says White.[10]

GET NOTICED

In corporate America, many companies say, "If you work hard and do your job well, you'll be rewarded." Sounds great in theory, but here's the rub: Management doesn't always notice and appreciate an employee's hard work.

Yet many women believe, erroneously and to their detriment, that if they just work harder, they'll get the same recognition as men.

Consider:

- Only 2 percent of women earn more than $50,000 a year.*
- Out of 4,012 people who were the highest-paid officers and directors in nearly 800 companies, only 19 were women— that's less than one-half of 1 percent.**
- In a study of division heads, assistant vice presidents, corporate secretaries, and other top jobs at 255 corporations, barely 5 percent of 9,293 employees were women.†
- Women executives, administrators, and managers often make only 70 percent of what men do.‡

There are, of course, a lot of reasons why many capable, hard-working women fail to score big money, top jobs, and corner offices—a crowded work force and sexist attitudes, to name a couple. But one major reason is that many women hold rigidly to the belief that if they simply work harder, they'll be rewarded with big money and top jobs (commonly called *waiting to be noticed*).

Often they believe, "Look, if I'm the best, and I'm the brightest, and I work the hardest, and I do the best-quality work around here, then the next time there is a promotion opportunity, I have to get it; there is no question," says Ronald C. Pilenzo, president of the Society for Human Resource Management. "And then when they don't, they're chagrined and extremely depressed.

"And if they ask the boss 'why?' Sometimes it's very difficult to articulate why because it really has nothing to do with competence and more to do . . . [with] how they relate to other people, how effective they are in getting things done, how effective they are in negotiating what they want," says Pilenzo.[14]

---

*U.S. Department of Commerce, Bureau of Census, "Advance Data from the March 1990 Current Population Survey," September 19, 1990.
**Jaclyn Fierman, "Why Women Still Don't Hit the Top," *Fortune*, July 30, 1990, p.40.
†Ibid.
‡U.S. Department of Labor, the Bureau of Labor Statistics, Table 5—Monthly Labor, 1990.

Recognize from day one that you *must* use strategies to make sure your superiors know you expect to advance in the company and that you intend to back up ambition with superior job performance. Most important, you need to make sure your efforts get noticed. The best way to do this is to master office politics and develop high-caliber interpersonal skills. (See Chapter 2.)

A warning: "Sure, competence is the key, but you also have to know how to play the game," says Carolyn Elman. "Women are learning that you don't just sit back and wait to be noticed."[15]

BUILD RAPPORT WITH MALE BOSSES AND CO-WORKERS

The problem: Rodney, your boss, pals around with another male employee in your department. Rodney and Scott play tennis and go to a lot of basketball games together. While your job performance has been excellent, you're afraid Rodney may promote Scott instead of you—just because they're friends.

How can you have a good rapport with male bosses and co-workers if you're female?

Many women feel men have an advantage in cultivating better relationships with male bosses. They believe opportunities to socialize outside the office turn into opportunities within the office. Here are some suggestions to prevent this from happening:

Don't Ignore the Obvious. "I don't think you have to do a lot of off-line activities if a boss is comfortable coming over to your desk and chatting and doing things like that," says David L. Bradford of Stanford. "The secret is to make your manager feel at ease with you in projects and discussions. If you sense a cool relationship, you can go in that person's office and say, 'Am I doing something that is getting in the way?'"[16]

Let's Go to Lunch. So what if the guys go to a basketball game once a month? Lunch is your passport to building and promoting better work relationships with male bosses and co-workers.

TIP

Know Which Myths to Confront

Question: If the battle isn't over, what myth do you think most women need to confront? Let's hear what the experts had to say:
Kate White, editor-in-chief of *Working Woman* Magazine:

The biggest problem a lot of women face lately is the myth that they are not 100 percent committed. There have been some studies that have indicated that because women may choose, at some point, to be mothers or leave work for a while, they are perceived as not being fully committed.

Men in companies, from what I've seen, don't view women as committed, 100 percent committed, the way they view some of the men who work for them. And that is a problem that women in corporations are coming up against—the glass ceiling. The reason they can't get beyond it is the perception that when it comes right down to it, women aren't going to stick with it.[17]

Carolyn Elman, executive director of the American Business Women Association:

The myth that you can have it all—that you can have a very successful career, family life, exercise, and serve gourmet meals and all that stuff that you read in magazines. I think it is very difficult, and I think it is a myth.[18]

Jo Foxworth, president of Jo Foxworth, Inc.:

The big thing to say to young women is the battle is *not* over by a long shot. So many of them feel that women have it made now, and there is practically no gender discrimination in business. And that just isn't true.

I hear them say, That was a problem of my mother's generation, not mine. Women are now permitted to do anything that they want.'

Well, sure, up to a point. But the line at that point is still just as firmly drawn as it ever was. And it is drawn at different points and places so that it is very hard to say where it is or determine where it might be.[19]

Constance Berry Newman, director of Office of Personnel Management.

If you work hard, are competent, and easy to get along with, you can get to the top of the ladder.[20] (It takes a lot more; you need to get noticed.)

Alma Baron, professor emeritus at the Management Institute School of Business at the University of Wisconsin:

I think the biggest hang-up women confront at work is the belief that they have a lower commitment to work than men. . . . Men seemingly feel that a woman's first commitment is to home and family, which in many instances it is, but they are able to deal with corporate responsibilities as well as home and family.[21]

Make it clear if you see a group of men going to lunch that you'd like to be included. Just say, "Can I join you for lunch?"

Another way to work your way into the lunch group is to ask a co-worker who is part of the "in" lunch group, "You know, you guys go out to lunch a lot. If you don't mind, I'd like to join you sometime." Next time they go to lunch, you co-worker friend may say, "Hey, let's ask Laurie to join us."

Friday Happy Hour. "Let's get a group up for Happy Hour," you say. "That sounds great," they say. Be careful, though. Happy Hours are frowned on in some organizations, and you don't want to be labeled the office lush, either. Play it safe—order bottled water or Pepsi.

Read the Sports Page. "Women tell me nothing helps like reading the sports pages and being intimately familiar with the sports world," says Ross Webber, a professor of management at the Wharton School. "Even if you don't play the sport, this can help you talk about it."[22]

But I Hate Talking Sports. "I once had a boss who was a bit of a chauvinist," says Kate White. "But one thing I discovered about him was that we each liked to read detective novels. . . . Later, I used it as an opportunity to drop off a copy of a book for him, strike up a conversation, and have a little small talk."[23]

That common interest helped White to develop a strong bond and good working relationship. "It allowed me to have the rapport with him I was afraid I wasn't going to get. He was naturally drawn to the young men in the office who talked sports.

"There was no way I was going to fake being interested in football and basketball, so I found other common denominators, detective novels and old movies."

The results? "Fabulous reviews . . . I think I delivered for him what he really wanted in an employee. I had several big promotions and several big salary increases," says White.[24]

But I Have to Pick My Kids Up from Day Care.   Join task forces, committees, and review groups. Act personable. You can have employee bonding without hanging out after work. Most opportunities for employee interaction help bosses and co-workers get to know you better.

Outside opportunities to associate with male managers and co-workers are important to advancement, but not as important as you might think. "I think most successful woman, when they move up the ladder, tend to remain themselves in terms of their own femininity, but how they gain the respect and attention of their peers and superiors is by being the best at what they do," says Dan Murphy, president of Corporate Dynamics.[25]

OVERCOME SPECIAL PROBLEMS OF WOMEN MANAGERS

"I think that if you're worried about being called a bitch, then you shouldn't be in management," says Marilyn Moats Kennedy, president of Career Strategies. "Management isn't a popularity contest—it's effectiveness. Why should people cooperate with you? Because it's in their best interests? Show them their own self-interest."[26]

As a woman manager, you want to be effective, not tough (unless it's necessary). Toughness here means using choke-collar techniques to gain control and results. But most employees respond better to sincerity, honesty, and fairness.

The easiest way to do this is to show quiet competence. Do this

---

TACTIC

Take an Assertiveness Training Course

"There is absolutely no excuse in the world for anybody in a work scene to be aggressive; that is, to humiliate people, to put them down, to be rude, to roll over them," says Thomas L. Quick, co-author of *The Ambitious Woman's Guide to a Successful Career* (AMACOM). "There is no excuse in the world to justify being aggressive."

But a woman manager must make it very clear to people she works with what she sees going on and how she feels about it, and the changes she wants.

"Assertiveness training helps you identify your needs and wants and express those needs and wants in a way that is acceptable to others. It's a form of communicating," says Quick.[28]

Courtesy should be extended to all in the workplace. "If you treat people as lower beings one time, they never forget it," says the University of Wisconsin's Alma Baron. "What people always remember about managers is: whether they treat them with respect or not."[29]

Good managers try to be assertive, not aggressive. The best way to do this is to take an assertiveness training course.

---

by acting confident, not cocky. And don't get hung up on whether male employees like you.

Don't play favorites, either. "The theory is men don't like to work for women because they think they won't do enough for their careers," says Kennedy.[27] Therefore, if you are a woman manager, make sure your people are getting promoted. Otherwise, the myth is a fact.

Show you care about your employees. Ask for input such as, "How do you feel about this idea, John?" Compliment good work. Don't be afraid to say, "John, I liked how you handled that report."

Strive to be an effective manager. Your goal is to win the respect of your employees. And if they like you, you're one lucky manager. But for some managers, being respected and liked might not be in the cards. Just be glad you're effective.

Tips for New Women Managers

Here are some suggestions to help you become a better manager for your company:

- Don't overconsult and let a group make basic decisions that you can make yourself.
- Don't try to run the ball all by yourself; don't hesitate to use your superiors for a resource.
- Find out the needs, concerns, and goals of your employees. Then link what you want to what they need.
- Find the best model of a manager in your organization, whether a man or a woman. Then model your behavior after that manager.
- Don't show favorites between male and female employees.
- Be helpful and supportive.
- Admit when you're wrong.
- Don't abuse your authority over employees whether they are men or women.
- Accept that some employees may resent you initially because they believe you don't deserve your position. (Be patient; they'll come around once you win their respect.)
- Nurture and appreciate your employees—people make the difference.
- Learn the skills of delegating, controlling, motivating, and co-ordinating employees. Those skills are the measure of a successful manager, whether you are a man or a woman.
- Give people credit; allow them to come forward and be recognized.

CONFRONT SEX AND RACE DISCRIMINATION

At some point in your career, expect to confront some form of discrimination. It might be as simple as missing a promotion. For the sake of argument, you're bright, talented and hard-working—and,

TACTIC

Can You Have a Fast-Track Career on 45 Hours a Week?

The problem is how to show corporate commitment, 14-hour days, out-of-town travel, and still manage a home . . . raise normal kids. So I asked Carolyn Elman, Alma Baron, Jo Foxworth, Constance Berry Newman, and Kate White: "Can a woman have a fast-track career on 45 hours a week?"

Carolyn Elman, executive director of the American Business Women Association:

> Yes, but I think you have to be real careful how you spend your time and spend it real wisely. And I also think you have to have a lot of support at home if you're married and have kids. Support at home is critical.
>
> I think it depends on the job. If you are talking about 30-year-old people, you are going to have the same resistance to 70-hour weeks whether they are male or female. There is resistance to spending 70 hours a week on the job.[30]

Alma Baron, professor emeritus at the Management Institute School of Business at the University of Wisconsin:

> No, I don't think so. Women on the fast track are participating in a balancing act and in most instances they have a very sympathetic husband or significant other.
>
> But I don't think working a 70-hour week is good, either. That means you can't get your work done.
>
> Unfortunately, this has been perpetuated year after year and generation to generation. A man doesn't have to give 70 hours unless he is totally incompetent.[31]

Kate White, editor-in-chief of *Working Woman* Magazine:

> I think some of the problem is how the workweek has expanded in recent years beyond what is reasonable. A lot of baby boomers are questioning these 70- and 80-hour weeks that they were bragging about only yesterday.
>
> Baby boomers are on the threshold of middle age and are asking, "All those hours were for what?" Not all of them got to the top. Many of them are plateauing. They haven't spent as much time with their families as they would have liked. And what have they got to show for it?

Maybe that question of a 45-hour week and a fast-track career won't be as significant 10 years from now because a 70-hour workweek won't be as common a situation in many fields. Maybe we will get back to shorter workweeks.

I see so many men and women alike saying, "I didn't get anything out of this." So I'd have to say it depends on the organization; if a man can get by with a 45-hour week, so can a woman.[32]

Jo Foxworth, president of Jo Foxworth, Incorporated:

It is hard to generalize and it is, of course, hard to say what kind of help she is getting at home. She might have a very understanding husband who pitches in—or children who are willing to help. Unfortunately, quite the opposite could be true.

Usually a woman is not able to relinquish her duties at home. A man has never been tied to all those tasks. Still, it is often assumed that it is the woman's job to look after the household, the food, the cleanliness, and the clothes for everybody.

Women in business often have a dual job and the most successful ones do not have a dual job—they have the help they need at home, usually. Or maybe—they don't even pretend their home life is a success.[33]

Constance Berry Newman, director of Office of Personnel Management for the U.S. government:

Although there is an emotional drain, the time drain on women with extra work at home isn't as bad as it used to be. Society is changing and there is more sharing of responsibilities between men and women, or at least there should be, in the home.

And there are more women contracting out some of their responsibilities such as employing housekeepers, shoppers, and using day care. If you look in the newspaper, there are more shopper services, housecleaning services.

So to the extent that women can get other people to do some of their jobs, they can use their time visiting with the children, and they don't have to be cleaning the house and doing the shopping, the easier it is for them to share a career and home. Unfortunately, the option of hiring outside help only works for people at those rungs of the ladder who can afford it.[34]

yes, you incorporate an individual advancement program such as *How to Make Your Boss Work for You* into your life.

But before you start screaming discrimination, you may need to look inward. "People have to be honest with themselves," says Constance Berry Newman. "They should review with themselves what their strengths and weaknesses are, how well they are doing the job, before they start pointing the finger at others (claiming discrimination).

"I advise people to be honest about what it is a job requires of them, what skills they have to do the job, and what they need to do to improve those skills," says Newman. "An *honest* evaluation shows whether they are doing the job properly, because sometimes people don't select you for other things because you're doing diddly-squat."[35]

So what do you do when you feel that you are being discriminated against? "I'm generally reluctant to recommend that people go dashing off to personnel offices and equal opportunity offices to complain because I don't know if you win that way," says Newman. "I think you win primarily by going directly to the person who is the problem, and sometimes you are not going to change them."[36]

Sit down with your boss and share your feelings about how you're being treated. This may get you nowhere, but some managers discriminate against women and minorities and don't even know they're doing it.

If that happens, "Confront the boss, whether it be personnel or the manager, and say, 'You know, I don't think I'm being treated fairly, and let me tell you why I don't think I'm being treated fairly,'" says Ronald Pilenzo.[37]

Try to discuss your concerns without alienating your boss. Keep your remarks focused. Resist saying, "I think you are sexually discriminating against me," or, "I think you are biased against women." "All that does is set people on edge—even if it is true," says Pilenzo.

Hopefully, your meeting works, but if it doesn't, you may have to go up the line to personnel or the equal opportunity office. But sometimes you exhaust your options at the company, not counting a lawsuit. "When this happens, you may need to move on," says Newman.[38]

Discrimination is a major obstacle, but you can rise above it. For

TACTIC

When is a Good Time to Have Children in a Fast-Track Career?

When it comes to career, one question women are asking is: When is the best time to have children? Early? Middle? Late? Never?

Alma Baron believes young women should work hard and make themselves practically indispensable to companies before they take time off to have children. "If a woman finishes school and has no experience and then stays home and has children, it becomes difficult for her to then enter the work force, especially in a position she feels qualified to handle," says Baron.[39]

On the other hand, having children in your 20s may be a shrewd strategy. "You come into your higher management jobs when your kids are in high school and college," says the American Business Women's Elman. "You have different problems when your kids are older, but you don't have the sick time, the real important stuff that prevents you from going to the office.

"A lot of problems that you have with teenagers can be dealt with after hours," says Elman. "But you have to deal with measles during work time."[40]

Perhaps the answer isn't early or late. "For a woman, I think there is really *no good* time to have children in a career," says Jo Foxworth. "But if I were pinned to the wall, I'd have to say—early. But then again, those early years are the years you position yourself for the really fast track, and if you are not there to be a real contender, then you've lost out."[41]

OK, but consider what Professor Ross Webber of Wharton said in Chapter 5: You need to position yourself in an organization by your early 30s if you intend to rise to the highest levels. But, ironically, many women intent on upper management choose their early and mid 30s to have children—just the time they should be positioning themselves for an ascent into upper management.

I hate to cop out, folks, but nobody but you can decide the best time to have kids. Ultimately, however, it will depend on your personal and professional goals and where you are in your career.

example, you might not make partner at one law firm because of discrimination. But at another law firm you make partner in 12 months. The goal is the same—only the location is different.

Don't get me wrong. Discrimination *IS* a very complicated, unfair career obstacle. My intention is not simplicity; but like other career obstacles you confront, if you exhaust your options, don't keep hitting your head against the wall. Cut your losses and change jobs.

DEAL WITH SEXUAL HARASSMENT

Of course, you are not so naive as to believe the problem will just go away. The first time you are sexually harassed by a boss, you have two choices. First, you can report the incident to human resources. Or, if you feel magnanimous, you can say, "I'm sure you know what you're doing is against the law. You probably wouldn't like it if I filed a grievance with human resources. Now let's get back to work, and—please don't let it happen again."

Giving a boss a break isn't always a good idea, though. You may lose ground with human resources if the boss continues to harass you. When you report your boss, they may view your grievance suspiciously. They may even ask, "Why did you wait so long to report these incidents?"

Refuse to be a victim of sexual harassment. Go through established channels first. Hopefully, they can resolve your problem. But if they can't, you may need to change jobs or see a lawyer.

Good news: More and more companies are coming down hard on offenders. (It's good policy, and harassment lawsuits are costly.) And they're pushing education to show what exactly is sexual harassment and why it's wrong.

HANDLE A SPOUSE WHO RESENTS YOUR INCOME

"I outearn my husband by almost $10,000 dollars a year," says Stephanie, an electrical engineer. "Gary is real sensitive about it, and it puts a lot of friction on our marriage."

Sounds like this guy suffers from low self-esteem. Maybe he resents Stephanie for his own perceived lack of success. Even if his wife got a job for minimum wage, it wouldn't solve the problem, however. People with low self-esteem will always find some other reason to complain.

While this sensitive problem couldn't possibly be resolved in one brief section, I still have two suggestions. (See section entitled "Dealing with people who envy your success" in chapter 1.)

First, keep finances separate. Now, this might not be advantageous for tax purposes (a married couple filling jointly is usually more advantageous), but the peace of mind may be worth it if your husband does not know all your details. A spouse can't complain about your spending if you keep your funds separate. Or you may want to share household expenses pro rata.

Another possibility is to build up a spouse's image with remarks like, "You are so good at your job," or "I'm so proud of you." And avoid ego-deflating remarks like, "Look at all this money I earned on my W-2."

AT A GLANCE

Despite gains, a glass ceiling *still* prevents many women from scoring jobs in middle and upper management. Here are some suggestions to help you break through the glass ceiling:

1. Check a company's track record for promoting women into management before you even accept a job offer.
2. Once you realize opportunities to move up are exhausted or for some reason never existed, consider changing jobs.
3. Recognize some myths about women might be fact. Plan your strategy accordingly.
4. Don't wait to be noticed.
5. Work at developing a special bond with your boss.
6. Beware that sex discrimination still exists big-time. It's not as obvious as it once was, but it's just as brutal because it is oh so subtle.

CHAPTER 6 AUTHOR INTERVIEWS

1. Kate White, September 11, 1990.
2. Ibid.
3. Carolyn Elman, August 28, 1990.
4. Constance Berry Newman, September 5, 1990.
5. Ibid.
6. Elman, August 28, 1990.
7. Newman, September 5, 1990.
8. Jo Foxworth, August 30, 1990.
9. Newman, September 5, 1990.
10. White, September 11, 1990.
11. Alma Baron, August 27, 1990.
12. White, September 11, 1990.
13. Newman, September 5, 1990.
14. Ronald C. Pilenzo, May 18, 1990.
15. Elman, August 28, 1990.
16. David L. Bradford, May 21, 1990.
17. White, September 11, 1990.
18. Elman, August 28, 1990.
19. Foxworth, August 30, 1990.
20. Newman, September 5, 1990.
21. Baron, August 27, 1990.
22. Ross Webber, May 21, 1990.
23. White, September 11, 1990.
24. Ibid.
25. Dan Murphy, May 16, 1990.
26. Marilyn Moats Kennedy, May 16, 1990.
27. Ibid.
28. Thomas L. Quick, May 15, 1990.
29. Baron, August 27, 1990.
30. Elman, August 28, 1990.
31. Baron, August 27, 1990.
32. White, September 11, 1990.
33. Foxworth, August 30, 1990.
34. Newman, September 5, 1990.
35. Ibid.
36. Ibid.
37. Pilenzo, May 18, 1990.
38. Newman, September 5, 1990.
39. Baron, August 27, 1990.
40. Elman, August 28, 1990.
41. Foxworth, August 30, 1990.

Chapter Seven

The Real Scoop on Being a Manager

''Get rid of the fat; get rid of your middle management,'' is one of the most popular themes in management conferences today.[1]

It's a *DIFFERENT* corporate world out there: mergers, cutbacks, work teams, quality management programs, global marketing, downsizing.

After years of being king, the corporate hierarchy is changing big-time.

So in this chapter we will focus on you, and how you can thrive as a manager in the age of downsizing.

Here's what you'll learn:

- How to break into middle management.
- How to make it into upper management.
- How to maximize your contribution to a work team.
- Why you need to focus on results and not always efforts.
- How to treat employees like human beings and still be effective.
- How to overcome special career problems of being a manager.

Yes, I can chew gum and manage the department at the same time.

HOW TO SUCCEED AS A MANAGER

An associate publisher of a prestigious business journal sent me an invitation to subscribe recently.

One key selling point was that the business journal is serious and substantial. Yes, that's true (it's a great magazine). But to prove that point, the associate publisher took some potshots at Ken Blanchard and Spencer Johnson's best-selling book, *The One Minute Manager*. (Berkeley Books)

For example, the associate publisher believes the practice of management is almost as complex as brain surgery, and that you wouldn't want a one-minute brain surgeon, would you?

With all due respect, I think the associate publisher missed the point. The fundamental concepts of management are simple. It's the practice of day-to-day management that's a challenge.

Here are some suggestions to help you succeed as a manager: Yes, they're simple but effective:

Seek Advice.   Flying solo can get you into trouble. Don't feel you have to do everything on your own. Most bosses, even the autocrats, want to see the job done right and on time. Don't hesitate to tap a knowledgeable brain inside or outside your company.

Press Your Boss for Objectives.   Make sure you are in agreement about your objectives before the period, quarter, or year begins. The biggest risk you can take in dealing with your boss is not to be clear on what she expects.

Know Your Resources.   Get the particulars. You must clarify authority, especially when it comes to budgets. Exceed it and you may be doomed. In a nutshell, find out the rules of the game before you start playing.

How Am I Doing?   People are funny. You might think you are doing a great job. The boss jokes with you. You work hard. Then comes performance appraisal time: KABOOM! You can get blown to bits.

As a manager, periodically ask how you are doing. You might have to reevaluate or discard some objectives. The moral here, obviously, is that you'd better learn your objectives. Goals get changed or revised, often without you knowing it, so you had better make sure the objectives you have for your job are the same objectives that your boss has for the job.

Ask for feedback: Pay attention to data that shows how well you're achieving objectives. Use timetables and ratios to gauge your managerial performance. And, of course, review and analyze your progress.

Get Managerial Freedom.   It's a real turnoff having a boss who constantly breathes down your back. To be effective, you need plenty of freedom to operate. Use human relations skills to cultivate a good working relationship with your boss. Once you win your boss's respect and trust, you'll likely find a nice balance between support and smothering. (Need a strategy to get your boss to leave you alone? See Chapter 3.)

Reward Performance.   Make sure your subordinates know how well they do their work while they do it. Reward someone for a job that is done well. Rewards aren't always money. A sincere compliment like "You did a good job on that project" goes a long way.

TACTIC

How to be a Better Manager

I asked five leading management authorities to fill in the blanks to the sentence, "I think managers should do more _____ and less _____." Here's what they had to say.

Philip B. Crosby, chairman of Philip Crosby Associates, Inc., and author of *Leading: The Art of Becoming an Executive* (McGraw-Hill) and the best-selling *Quality Is Free* (McGraw-Hill):

> I think most managers should do more listening and less talking. Workers understand the job better than anybody. Listen to them. Give them the opportunity to tell their problems.
>
> Talk to workers and they'll tell you what to do when you have a problem. Management never does that. When the boss has a meeting, he or she talks as long as they want to talk. And when they quit talking the meeting is over.[2]

Greta Cotler, manager of professional product development at the American Society for Training and Development:

> I think managers should do more motivating and less controlling. It's very important to motivate the people who report to you. You must make them think that their work is worthwhile and that they are part of a team.
>
> What doesn't work is a very controlling manager looking over someone's shoulder, all the time, trying to tell someone exactly the way to do a job.
>
> Managers need to give employees a sense of what is the bottom line, the final product, and a sense that things will be revised. And they need to give their employees the freedom to figure out the best way to do a task.[3]

H. Kurt Christensen, of the J. L. Kellogg Graduate School of Management at Northwestern University:

> I think managers should concentrate on the substance of other people's comments and be less concerned with political posturing. In spite of America's serious competitive problems, I'm still surprised with how frequently the "not invented here" syndrome and other personal considerations derail otherwise constructive suggestions that people have.[4]

Dr. Craig Dreilinger, president of the Dreiford Group, a Bethesda, Maryland–based management consulting firm:

> Most managers should do more managing and less going to consultants and others and training to figure out how to manage.
>
> We have created a cadre of managers in corporate America that are less sure of themselves than they were 15 years ago. . . . We have convinced those managers, management gurus that we are, that we have the true wisdom, the knowledge, and the insights of how to manage and that we can tell them how to empower, how to innovate, how to manage change, and everything except how to do root canal.
>
> Somewhere along the way, many management consultants have lost sight of what it is we are trying to do. I see managers all over corporate America that are less sure than they should be and less willing to trust their gut instincts.[5]

George S. Odiorne, a senior research associate at Eckerd College Resource Institute, and author of the *Human Side of Management* (Lexington Books) and *How Managers Make Things Happen:* (Prentice Hall)

> I think most managers should do more walking around, more talking to people, more asking questions, answering questions, and interacting with people and looking at things. Being one-minute managers.
>
> And I think they should do less sitting on their cans in the office and less acting like bureaucrats.[6]

Too many bosses fail to compliment good work. Don't be like them.

Train Your Replacement.   Your advancement can slow to a halt if there is no one to replace you. It's usually self-defeating to avoid training someone because you fear that person wants your job. Not having someone to replace you can inhibit your advancement. After a while, you may become unpromotable.

MANAGE YOURSELF

Many people think the job of a manager *begins* by managing other people and tasks. Actually it doesn't. Effective managers know the job really begins by managing *themselves*.

Before you can effectively manage others, you MUST be able to manage your own life personally and professionally. Here's a recap of skills to manage yourself and where they're taught in your advancement program.

Chapter	Managers Need to:
Chapter 1	Deal with success and failure
Chapter 2	Master office politics
Chapter 3	Cultivate interpersonal skills
Chapter 4	Improve conversation and public speaking skills
Chapter 5	Overcome career obstacles
Chapter 6	Promote and develop women
Chapter 7	Become an effective manager
Chapter 8	Avoid getting fired
Chapter 9	Manage job stress
Chapter 10	Build health, energy, and stamina

HOW TO HANDLE THE POOR PERFORMER

"When there is a problem, I try to determine if a person can do the job and doesn't want to do it. Or if he can't do the job and needs training," says Charles W. Coxwell, a captain with the U.S. Army.

"Then I ask myself, 'Can he do the job? Does he know how to do it? If he doesn't know how to do it, can he learn to do it? Or is he not doing the job, but he knows how to do it.'

"The person who can do the job and doesn't want to do it needs more severe measures than someone who can't do the job but wants to do it. So when someone is trying, I nurture him with training and retraining."

With the other one the Army has to draw the line. "You're either in or out," says Coxwell. "The Army generally gives everybody a

30 to 90–day probation period to turn around. In the military, the competition is so stiff that there is little room for failure to progress."[7]

When you confront an employee about performance, take a lesson from the U.S. Army. Keep your remarks short and constructive. Focus on training and development and on what you can do together to solve the problem. Help people come up with their own solutions.

Poor performance isn't always a sign of incompetence. Often it's part of the learning curve. You need to deal firmly and quickly with skill deficiencies and basic personality faults, though.

Here are some tips to coach poor performers.

Do

- Rehabilitate and educate.
- Focus on solutions.
- Offer the employee an opportunity to explain and save a little face.
- Offer constructive advice.
- Avoid nitpicking petty weaknesses.

Don't

- Scapegoat.
- Rant or rave.
- Get hung up on punishing when someone makes a mistake.
- Raise your voice.
- Make derogatory remarks that destroy confidence.

HOW TO GIVE BETTER PERFORMANCE APPRAISALS

"I think most performance appraisals are useless because they are all beige and vanilla," says Philip B. Crosby, a management consultant.[8] Crosby believes employees need to participate in the pro-

TACTIC

Be A Trainer

Engineers know engineering. Accountants know accounting. And salespeople know selling. Superior technical skills like these—plus seniority—get people promoted into management.

But often these technically trained people have had little or no management training (Management 101 if they were lucky). Even though their jobs require them to train subordinates, they might be ill-equipped to do so.

Nothing is more frustrating than being told to do something and getting bad instructions. (I'm not talking about hooking up your VCR to the television.)

Here are some hints on giving better instructions and explanations to subordinates:

Use Examples.   Examples cement the ambiguous and make clear things you know inside and out but the other person doesn't know.

Explain Logic.   Make sure the people you train understand a project's logic. They will be happier and you'll save the department time.

Use Diagrams, Drawings, and Flowcharts.   Visual aids help people grasp complex topics faster. They don't have to spend hours spinning their wheels when the logic is spelled out.

Give Step-by-Step Instructions.   Remember, your role is to instruct and teach people how to do their jobs. When they fail, you fail. As a result, even if you think you're talking down to them, don't rush through instructions! Most important, don't assume they always know what to do.

Follow up.   Check back with employees to appraise samples of their work or to ask if they have any questions. Do not assume subordinates know what they're doing just because they haven't asked any questions.

cess actively. He thinks employees should fill out a form that gives them an opportunity to say (1) what they think their job really is, (2) how they feel about it, and (3) what suggestions they have for the company.

"The boss does the same thing," says Crosby. "Then they sit down with an open confidential agreement and talk about these points."

During the appraisal, "you don't want to say things like, 'I don't think you are energetic enough,' or 'Your mind is somewhere else.' You can't do much about those things. Instead, focus on specifics such as how well that person does his or her job, builds interpersonal relationships, and other issues.

"Then the employee has the opportunity to agree or disagree. This allows a boss to get a better understanding of the employee as a person. And the employee gets things to work on," says Crosby.[9]

Sounds good to me. But there are two more points I'd like to add. First, use current time when you evaluate performance. This allows you to focus on what the employee can do *now* and how well that person is doing it.

Second, don't get so hung up on weaknesses that you shatter someone's self-confidence. Too much negative feedback can cause an employee to feel extra psychological pressure. That pressure may cause that person to miss deadlines and do substandard work. Remember, you want to correct the poor performance, not perpetuate it.

Here are some other tips for reviewing subordinates:

- Just measure performance.
- Focus on strengths instead of weaknesses.
- Don't tell someone she has a future with the company if she doesn't.
- Build on strengths with new training.
- Don't use a bell curve to rate all employees in your department. (In a well-run department, most employees can be rated above average.)

MONEY TALKS

When it comes to the bottom line, some efforts to keep salaries in control backfire. Your company may lose a fortune in training costs, recruiting costs, absenteeism, and sick time. (See Chapter 11 for more details.)

Don't be a miser. While money doesn't always motivate employees, it still keeps many employees from looking for new jobs.

Here are tips to retain good employees and keep the bottom line in check:

- Know the difference between, "We reward performance," and, "We are cheap, cheap, cheap!"
- Avoid discussing money during performance appraisals.
- Play fair. Don't pass off a cost-of-living raise as a merit raise.
- Monitor salaries paid by competitors.
- Pay above-average wages for good performance.
- Don't promise more money and benefits than you can deliver.
- Resist taking benefits away from employees. When you make employees pay for benefits such as health insurance that were previously fringe benefits, it's bad for morale.

USE PARTICIPATIVE MANAGEMENT

I asked George S. Odiorne, "What is the real form of participation?" "It begins at the start of every quarter," he told me. "Every manager and every subordinate discuss what they are going to produce in terms of objectives."[14]

"Then they ask questions like, 'What would you like to produce?' 'What are your hopes?' 'What are your plans?' 'What are your dreams?' And the boss confirms that with a memo which he signs off. During the quarter, he offers help anytime he is asked.

"At the end of the quarter, he discusses your work and what plans you have for the next quarter. How well did you do it? What can you do better? Did you accomplish less than you said you

What Managers Get Wrong about Employees

Question: "What do you think managers get wrong about employees?"

Philip B. Crosby, chairman of Philip Crosby Associates, Inc.:

I think managers tend to think their employees are not as smart as they are. Very few people can recognize talent when they see it. You can look great as a manager if you find great people and develop them.[10]

George S. Odiorne, a senior research associate at Eckerd College Resource Institute:

The biggest misconception is that their employees are lazy and not as committed as they are. The people at the top say, 'What are those people doing? Why are they doing it? What are they contributing? and How do we get rid of them?'[11]

H. Kurt Christensen of the J. L. Kellogg Graduate School of Management at Northwestern University:

Many managers assume that employees don't really want to improve the effectiveness and the efficiency of their company's operations. But companies lose a lot of valuable input by not responding constructively to suggestions that are made by their employees in good faith.

Japanese companies, on the other hand, are very effective in making use of suggestions of people at all levels to improve performance. That has been an important contributor to their success in many industries. We need to follow their lead.[12]

Dr. Craig Dreilinger, a clinical psychologist and president of the Dreiford Group:

The notion that managers can change employees by spending huge sums of money on management consultants, management consulting firms, or corporations is ludicrous. . . . So much of the work we do in corporate American is based on the belief that somehow consultants can fundamentally change people. But people make choices to change; we don't change them.[13]

STRATEGY

Know Your Management Style

Let's talk about your leadership style as a manager. Rensis Likert, former director of the Institute for Social Research, developed a universal theory of leadership.*

Likert's theory consisted of these four management styles:

System 1—Exploitive Autocrat. Manager determines what to do. Next, manager decides which employees will do job. Then manager specifies how and when it will be done. Threats or punishment occur if employees fail to complete work as assigned.

System 1 management has little confidence or trust in employees. Not surprisingly, managers and employees share a low level of trust. Many exploitive autocrats focus solely on the company's bottom line.

System 2—Benevolent Autocratic. Boss still makes decisions, but employees have greater freedom and flexibility to do their jobs— if they follow company protocol.

Benevolent autocratic leaders take a more paternalistic approach than exploitive autocrats. For example, a benevolent autocrat might say, "Do a great job on the Morgan account, and I'll take care of you raise time."

Use caution when dealing with System 2 leaders; there is often a low level of trust between employees and management.

System 3—Consultive. Employees discuss work-related matters with management before goals are established and decisions are made. They also have considerable freedom to make decisions about how work is to be done. A consultive manager might say, "Mike, what are your thoughts about Glass Financial Corporation, before *I* make the decision to accept them as a client?"

System 3 management tends to rely on rewards (not punishment) to motivate employees. As a result, the level of trust between employees and management is fairly high.

---

*Rensis Likert, *New Patterns of Management* (New York: McGraw-Hill, 1961), pp. 222–28.

System 4—Participative Team.   Likert liked this one best. Employees take part fully in the process of establishing goals and making job-related decisions. Managers display supportive (not threatening or patronizing) conduct when issues are discussed.

This style works best when the whole organization is participative and work is done in a series of overlapping groups. A leader acts as a link between the group and other units in the organization (often called the *linking pin* theory). Since knowledge power often takes precedence over authority power, decision making is pervasive at all levels in the enterprise.

would? If there was a difference between what you said you were going to do and what you did? Was it your fault? Was it my fault? Was it beyond the control of both of us? How can we do better next quarter?'' says Odiorne.[15]

''Companies can get a lot of good public relations by having Tom Peters write about them in his books,'' (*Thriving on Chaos* [Knopf] and *In Search of Excellence* [Harper & Row]) continues Odiorne. ''But when it comes to many companies, he goes out and describes things (actual amount of employee participation in major decisions) that really aren't happening.''[16]

Odiorne also believes that many companies pay lip service to participative management. ''They really don't want people participating,'' he said.

Victoria Tashjian, a vice president with Wick and Company, agrees. ''Companies are now getting into various quality circles and employee involvement programs. Employees are asked to give their opinions, but often what they suggest or would like to do is not really used. . . . People become discouraged when their opinions are discarded,'' says Tashjian.

''So we go through the motions. We have the quality circles and have employee involvement meetings, but management often reverts to the old style of management and makes the decisions,'' says Tashjian.[17]

The Caste System in Corporate America

Generally, in a large traditional organization, there are three levels of managers. If it has been a while since you had your last management course, here's a review:

Top Managers. President, chief executive officer (CEO), vice president, executive directors, and so on. Leaders who are responsible for providing the overall direction of the firm.

Middle Managers. They coordinate programs and activities. They carry out general goals. Those goals are usually identified by top management.

Lower-level Managers. Supervisors manage employees who work in operations each day.

Moral: Companies, put your money where you say your participative management is.

HOW TO BREAK INTO MIDDLE MANAGEMENT

For better or worse, you are responsible for your own career development.

The following are some suggestions to help you break into middle management.

Pick the Right Organization. "Go with a well-run company," says Odiorne. "Don't go with something that is screwed up. Stay away from savings and loans and banks these days. They are troubled businesses."

"Stay out of the finance industry if you want to be a manager. Don't go with the brokerage firms because they are loaded with technicians rather than managers, and you won't learn any management from them.

STRATEGY

How to Get Back on the Fast Track Once You Plateau

The problem: You're caught in middle-management purgatory, you've had the same job for years, and your prospects for advancement are practically nonexistent. Can you get back on the fast track once you plateau?

"The only difference between a rut and a grave is the dimensions," says Philip Crosby. "I think companies peg people who haven't been promoted in years as not having a future."

Crosby advises that you change jobs if you find yourself in the same situation. "But first, get your act together."[18]

You might wonder how to revive your management career if you can't change jobs. "In most situations, getting back on the fast track is a possibility," says Christensen. "I think it is harder to do in large companies than in a smaller organization, but it's possible if you're able to get visibility by taking on a special assignment and handling it with distinction."[19]

It's a big challenge to get back on the fast track once you plateau. But with a positive attitude, lots of determination, and a desire to make a superior contribution, anything is possible.

"If you want to learn management, work for a well-run company where you work for a good boss," says Odiorne.[20]

Learn Your Job Quickly. "Make up your mind you are going to work your tail off," says Philip Crosby. "I'm often asked how to get noticed at work. I tell them, 'Find out what it is they want you to do and do it better than anybody ever did it, and you'll be chairman in six months!' Unfortunately, very few people do that."[21]

Understand What Is Expected. The key to success is to understand the requirements," says Crosby. "*Find out* what you and your department are expected to do, and concentrate on getting those things done promptly, correctly, and on time. That gets noticed!"[22]

STRATEGY

Shortcuts to Break into Upper Management

Whether you work in a huge law firm like Skadden, Arps, Slate, Meagher & Flom, or at General Motors Corporation, there will *always* be upper management. Here are some suggestions to help you score a top job in upper management.

1. History Repeats Itself.   Find out what background and career route have been successful in the past. For example, if you are going to work for Procter & Gamble Co., you either go into marketing or forget it. "Nobody ever made it to the top at Procter & Gamble out of manufacturing," says Eckerd college's George S. Odiorne."[23]

"A plant manager might earn $75,000 by the time he's 60. Who needs it? If you want to get to the top, get into the marketing training program.

"And if you're not a chemist or a chemical engineer at Du Pont, forget it. It's like being in the navy and getting seasickness, or joining the air force and hoping to get to the top if you are afraid of heights.

"If you are going to work for one of the big stockbroker firms like Goldman Sachs, get a master's degree in finance. Don't come in with something like human resources, you'll just be making coffee for the rest of them," says Odiorne.[24]

2. Do You Really Need an MBA?   I won't lie to you. An MBA helps. It is going to get you through some doors initially. It will get you into the track meet, but it won't help you run faster. But it will get you in the starting blocks, off the gun. After that, it's office politics and high performance.

3. Plan and Replan.   You're judged by your plans and how they achieve results. "No plan ever stands on its own until the first stumbling block is hit, then you have to replan the plan," says Charles W. Coxwell. "You have to constantly replan. And then you need to communicate changes in the plan without confusing people."[25]

4. Deliver the Basics.   No matter how you look at it, success as a manager is judged by factors such as earning a profit, reducing costs, increasing market share, and so on.

5. Think Strategically. "Today, you really need to understand what the business of the company is and what the company really looks at from a marketing point of view," says Greta Cotler. To make it into upper management, "you must think strategically about what the company's and organization's needs are."[26]

6. Don't Set Yourself Up to Derail. "Recognize that the competition is extremely stiff," says Victoria Tashjian. "In our workshops, we get people to ask, 'What are my own potential derailment factors?' Those factors will be different for different people. . . . In middle management, derailment tends to be caused by (1) the individual, (2) poor interpersonal relationships, (3) performance problems, (but a lot of times you can still be a good performer and still derail), (4) not being able to think strategically, (5) not having the right image—particularly for women."[27]

7. Get Assessment Feedback. "The best thing any middle manager can do to help them get past the middle-management stage is to get some assessment feedback on themselves," says Tashjian.

"Research shows that people who derail did not get honest feedback about themselves or they got the feedback and they didn't do anything about it."[28]

You can appraise yourself or use outside testing. (A warning: People tend to shy away from that kind of experience. It might reveal too much.) Learn what your strengths and weaknesses are. Next, make a plan to work on areas that need development.

8. Books Are Mentors, Too. "The biggest problem I have had with my middle managers over the years was getting them to read," says Philip Crosby. "They've got to read *The Wall Street Journal* and business magazines. They have to read professional magazines, and not just rely on Dan Rather to tell them about the world.

"That is hard work, and they bottom out very early, particularly professional managers that run specific departments like quality control and engineering. They get so wrapped up in their particular thing that they don't learn about managing, what is going on in the world, new technological advances, and they never become prevention oriented, they just become reactive," says Crosby.[29]

Ask your boss what is expected of you. "If bosses don't tell you, go ask them," says Odiorne. If they don't know, get out."[30]

Get Things Done through Others.   Some managers never learn that the job of a manager is to get things done through others. They don't sit down with their people and get their input. Nor do they allow them to be accountable and responsible for carrying out decisions.

To keep your career on the fast track, promote teamwork. Victoria Tashjian once told her staff, "I'm going to be depending on you a lot. You all have something to contribute here, and let's look at me as the coach of the team. I'm here to make sure you have the resources. Let's sit down and think things out as a team and come up with a game plan."[31]

Learn Team Management Skills.   You bet company hierarchy is changing, but there will always be corner offices. "Supervisors who survive the reduction or elimination of first-line supervisory positions will have a new kind of a job," says Glenn Varney, director of the masters of organization development program at Bowling Green State University. "They are going to be very different people, they're not going to be line-type managers. They are going to be responsible for helping teams and other groups of people in the organization. They'll be coordinating.

"So before they move up, they are going to have to learn how to manage teams," says Varney. "I would say American managers, in general, are not very qualified in the management skills required to manage teams," he added.[32]

SPECIAL CAREER PROBLEMS OF MANAGERS

Baby Buster Blues.   You're bright, talented, and fresh out of school. One problem, though. Your first job in management just isn't challenging. The company expects you to pay your dues.

My advice is to resist the temptation to quit. You could change jobs for a more immediately challenging position. But what often happens is that managers, as they advance up the company ladder, receive more challenging and satisfying managerial assignments. So, bite the bullet and focus on the future. Proving yourself goes with the territory.

Companies, if you have problems with turnover, give your new managers opportunities to communicate with higher level managers. It also helps to have a higher level manager, as well as an immediate supervisor, evaluate young managers, too.

Too Much Competition for Top Managerial Jobs.   "Managerial skills and technical competence in today's environment are the smallest percentage of how you move up in the 1990s," says Dr. Craig Dreilinger of the Dreiford Group. "The larger percentage is doing your politics and being in the right place at the right time."[33]

Here are the attributes that Dreilinger believes you need to score a middle- or upper-management job:

Attribute Required to Break into Management	Percent
Being an outstanding performer and exceptional manager	25%
Mastering office politics	35
Being in the right place at the right time	40
	100%

Not Knowing What Employees Want.   Most employees want: more information about what's going on, more freedom to do their jobs; more say; more guidance; honest feedback, no promises that can't be met; you to notice and reward hard work; less over-the-shoulder treatment; more money; and more support.

Different Management Styles.   Many managers get promoted into management based on seniority or superior technical skills. But once in management, interpersonal skills play a big part in future career development. For example, you may have a boss who is very autocratic and you're more team oriented. The boss may try to get you to mold your style to be just like him. No quick fix for this problem. Just use human relations training to improve your relationship with your boss. (See Chapter 3.)

Is This Loyalty, Anyway?   Many workaholic bosses work way past quitting time. This creates a problem: Many subordinate managers feel compelled to work longer hours because they don't want to be stereotyped as clock-watchers who leave before the boss.

Some workaholic bosses consider time spent at the office, not work accomplished, to be loyalty. Unfortunately, what happens is people put in long hours, but they don't use those hours to make a bigger contribution or become more effective.

Before you accept certain jobs, it doesn't hurt to find out if the environment is autocratic. If it is, you might want to find a job in a more participatory environment.

AT A GLANCE

It takes strategy and talent to break into middle and upper management in an age of downsizing. Here's a recap of significant points contained in this chapter:

- Don't underestimate your employees.
- Managers are responsible for their own career development.
- Poor performance isn't always a sign of incompetence. Often it is just part of the learning curve.
- Performance appraisals should focus on current time.
- It's possible for derailed middle managers to get back on the fast track.
- Know the difference between, "We reward performance" and, "We are cheap, cheap, cheap!"
- Realize that many supposedly team-oriented or participative companies may only pay lip service to participative management.

CHAPTER 7   AUTHOR INTERVIEWS

1. George S. Odiorne, September 21, 1990.
2. Philip B. Crosby, September 26, 1990.
3. Greta Cotler, October 9, 1990.
4. H. Kurt Christensen, October 9, 1990.
5. Craig Dreilinger, October 10, 1990.
6. Odiorne, September 21, 1990.
7. Charles W. Coxwell, September 26, 1990.
8. Philip B. Crosby, September 26, 1990.
9. Ibid.
10. Ibid.
11. Odiorne, September 21, 1990.
12. Christensen, October 9, 1990.
13. Dreilinger, October 10, 1990.
14. Odiorne, September 21, 1990.
15. Ibid.
16. Ibid.
17. Victoria Tashjian, September 24, 1990.
18. Crosby, September 26, 1990.
19. Christensen, October 9, 1990.
20. Odiorne, September 21, 1990.
21. Crosby, September 26, 1990.
22. Ibid.
23. Odiorne, September 21, 1990.
24. Ibid.
25. Coxwell, September 26, 1990.
26. Cotler, October 9, 1990.
27. Tashjian, September 24, 1990.
28. Ibid.
29. Crosby, September 26, 1990.
30. Odiorne, September 21, 1990.
31. Tashjian, September 24, 1990.
32. Glenn Varney, September 28, 1990.
33. Dreilinger, October 10, 1990.

Chapter Eight

Don't Come Monday!

Friday, 4:45 P.M. Something is up. Something big. He calls you at your desk.

"I need to see you in my office," he says. This is it. "Have a seat."

He closes the door. Everyone must be watching. Everyone must know. This can't be happening.

He reclines in his high-back leather chair, and oh, he gives you that look. That look that says, "This is harder on me than it is on you."

Damn. You're going to be fired. That's right. Fired. The long hours you gave him, the effort you put in, the Cross pen you gave him for Christmas—all for nothing.

He is going to fire you; you will never find another job again. People will gossip. Your family will think less of you. You owe money, lots of it.

"As you know, we have been watching your performance quite closely," he says. "You make mistakes. Your productivity is not what we expect, and, quite frankly, you don't seem to care about your job."

Here it comes.

"We are going to have to let you go."

With that, life as you know it ends. You will never work again! Your friends will desert you! You will eat in soup kitchens!

Or, you pick yourself right up and you begin again.

Losing a job is not the end of the world. Not even close.

Hey, just about everybody has been fired once. Ease some of your pain with the knowledge that many successful people have also been fired from jobs.

Once you've been fired, you've joined the likes of Linda Ellerbee, Helen Gurley Brown, Barbara Walters, Lee Iacocca, Andrew Grove, and even General Douglas MacArthur. Talk-show hostess Sally Jessy Raphael was axed from 18 different jobs before she found her niche in front of a national television audience.

You may be fired from at least one job during your career. More than 2.5 million Americans were classified as job losers because of firings and permanent layoffs for the month of October 1990 according to the U.S. Department of Labor, Bureau of Labor Statistics (*Employment and Earnings* Table A-41, November 1990). With numbers like that, it is easy to see why there isn't the same social stigma attached to a firing that once existed.

That still does not make it something you should look forward to. It should also not be something that comes as a complete surprise. There are warning signals, clear signs of big trouble, that you must watch for throughout your career.

WHY IT HAPPENS

In Dad's generation, if someone got fired, it was usually because he was incompetent, insubordinate, or just plain deserved it. These days, thanks to a volatile economy and a crowded labor force, devoted workers get fired, too.

Here's how:

1. Poor performance. You are not doing what is expected of you.
2. Bad attitude. You hate your job or your boss or your workplace. It shows. It always does.

3. Personality conflicts. Your boss doesn't like you. You don't like your boss.
4. The company is in trouble, can't afford you, and lays you off.

IS IT REALLY POOR PERFORMANCE?

"The covenant we all thought we had 30 years ago was: 'If you keep your nose clean and do a good job, you can retire and get a gold watch,' " says Thomas R. Horton, chairman and CEO of the American Management Association. "Nowadays you may be told on a Friday afternoon, 'That's it, Charlie!' "[1]

"Sometimes management makes the mistake of promoting people into positions they're not really ready for," says Peter Kurth, a human resources executive with Barnett Bank.[2]

Let's explore four performance problems that can lead to early departure from a company.

Wrong Fit.   Friction occurs when employers expect inexperienced employees to complete job assignments that are routinely beyond their technical training and ability.

This is a common problem of entry-level employees. Why? Employers often expect them to have job skills that weren't taught in college.

Witness Linda, who thought she was ready for the rigors of the real world when she graduated from college. Her first job was as a management trainee at a major department store:

"My boss did not have the time to train me. She wanted me to come into the job and already know what was going on. She wanted me to keep up with other employees who had years of experience.

"There were a lot of things that she expected me to do, for the first time, that I didn't have enough job knowledge to carry out. I couldn't do the job. I made mistakes. My work was seldom done on time. Then I got fired."

STRATEGY

How to Get Your Boss to Train You

Are you in over your head? Here's how to rise above a boss who isn't training:

- When you don't know how to do something, ask a knowledgeable superior or co-worker how to do it. Don't waste time spinning your wheels in an effort to teach yourself. Be persistent. Keep asking questions until you know how to do the assignment.
- Schedule a conference with your boss. Be honest; admit your lack of job knowledge. Enlist the boss's help to get it.
- Ask a supervisor to appraise samples of your work to see if it's up to par.
- Ask for interim minievaluations. Most bosses will give extra feedback if you prod them.
- Read employee and industry manuals.
- Take a self-study course.
- Tap vendors, professionals, libraries, and other sources for job knowledge.
- Request a transfer to a more suitable job.
- If none of the above suggestions work, *Change Jobs!*

Asking Too Much.   Sam, a recent business graduate and restaurant manager, had his district manager say, ''Increase sales by 20 percent over last year's figures, or look for another job.''

Twenty percent! The odds were firmly stacked against him. Two new restaurants had opened near his restaurant.

Sam tried everything. Specials, Gimmicks. Advertising. After a year, he had raised sales by 10 percent. He thought his boss would be grateful. His boss was furious.

Sam was fired.

Some managers expect their employees to accomplish unrealistic work assignments.

TIP

Confront a boss with unrealistic goals. Ask for more attainable goals. If the boss is flexible, you might salvage your job.

No matter how much overtime and extra effort employees put in, they usually can't satisfy bosses who don't want to be satisfied. If by sheer fortitude they accomplish unreasonable goals, their employer will probably reward them with yet another unreasonable assignment.

So what's a frustrated employee to do? If you ever find yourself continually confronting absurd employer expectations, you have no choice but to change jobs.

Incompetence.   Be honest. Maybe you were not the perfect choice for the job. Maybe you were the worst choice for the job. Plenty of marginal employees skate by for years. But as the marketplace becomes increasingly competitive, it becomes much less tolerant of incompetence.

Can you do your job? Can you do it well? If not, you may be in danger of losing it.

Insubordination.   If you make a habit of failing to follow instructions or talking back, you are making yourself incredibly expendable. Face it. You are an employee. You get paid to do what your boss tells you to do—exactly what your boss tells you to do.

Barbara, a research assistant, knew more than her boss. She knew she knew more than her boss, and she let him know it. He gave her an assignment to research one aspect of an environmental problem. She turned in a 40-page paper on something else. Her paper was beautiful. But it wasn't what he wanted.

"I think you know a little too much," he told her as she was being dismissed. ''But the one thing you haven't learned is that the boss is the boss.''

YOU'VE GOT AN ATTITUDE PROBLEM

A bad attitude is one sure way to get fired. Companies may put up with a lot of things, but a bad attitude isn't one of them. Here's how you make yourself an easy target:

Sorry, But You Asked for It If You . . .

- Publicly bad-mouth the company.
- Mention starting a (uh-oh) union.
- Let personal problems affect your job performance.
- Poison office morale.
- Cheat on your expense account.
- Botch up assignments.
- Get romantically involved with a co-worker.
- Resist learning new tasks.
- Become the office troublemaker.
- Act lazy, disorganized, or indifferent.
- Do anything flagrantly dishonest.
- Come late, take long lunches, or leave early.
- Have a drinking problem.
- Routinely decline overtime and out-of-town travel assignments.

WHEN DALE CARNEGIE FAILS

Hey, wait a minute. Not all firings are due to poor performance or a bad attitude. ''Nearly 75 percent of all firings are political in nature,'' says Marilyn Moats Kennedy, president of Career Strategies.[3] Here's how they happen:

The Classic Personality Clash.   It is like a badly mixed cocktail made with incompatible ingredients. Some personalities do not mesh. If you make a martini with kahlua instead of vermouth, you have one bad-tasting martini. The same is true if you cross a high-strung, detail-oriented boss with an assistant who is outgoing, enthusiastic, and full of new ideas.

Co-Workers Can Sabotage Your Chances for Success.   Of course, others might be contributing to your impending downfall. It happens all the time. One worker sees a chance to move ahead at your expense. He or she may not like you. It is commonplace for co-workers to use unfair guerilla warfare techniques. Others might spread rumors or isolate you in an effort to destroy your morale and neutralize you within the organization.

Some employees rattle off remarks to their bosses about co-workers in order to enhance their standing in the company. "David is looking for another job," one might say. "I like Dana, but I just can't afford to go out with her for those two-hour lunches she takes," another might offer. Or, "I'd ride to work with Sandy, but she drinks too much for me to feel comfortable with her at the wheel."

An isolation campaign may occur gradually or start in full force on your first day on a new job. Your co-workers may act uncooperative, indifferent, or even hostile toward you. They might not go to lunch with you. They might leave you out of company-related, nonwork activities such as a bowling league or softball team. You may hear remarks from third parties who tell you that your co-workers consider you stuck-up, snobby, cocky, or egotistical.

Employees who sabotage another co-worker's progress sometimes do so because they want a co-worker to conform to the status quo. In other words, an inefficient group of workers might loathe someone who is productive, competent, and perceived as being the boss's pet. They don't want someone to be different. They are afraid of being outworked and outclassed by the productive worker.

Problem Bosses.   He's the boss. That does not necessarily make him the smartest, friendliest, and most well-adjusted person on earth. It just makes him the boss. And his quirks can make working together a challenge.

Some workers may intimidate an insecure boss with their superior credentials and competence. If you are so good, you might take your boss's job.

Some managers abuse power to prop their fragile egos. So they might hold subordinates back or make their jobs unpleasant.

Other bosses project anger at innocent parties. Instead of confronting their problems, some managers blow off steam at their employees for something totally unrelated to the matter at hand.

Different Lifestyles.   He's a born-again Christian. You're not. Or she's a fitness fanatic, you're a chain smoker. Or maybe he's a heavy-drinking, pot-smoking rebel and you're a member of Young Republicans.

Usually, people learn to work together in spite of their differences. But there are some bosses who want all of their subordinates to be just like them. They do not tolerate individualism.

Some managers believe what employees do outside the office is as important as their performance on the job. While firing someone because of his or her lifestyle is against the law in many states, employers will often cite another reason to support a firing.

CASUALTIES OF THE BOTTOM LINE

They always say it. "Times are tough." So tough, they have to eliminate your department. Or just eliminate you. The economy can be very unforgiving: When it comes to saving your job or the company, which do you think the corporation is going to choose?

Here are some ways a company can discard you to improve its bottom line:

The Merger.   In comes the new company with visions of glory and prosperity. Yes, things will change, they say, but only for the better.

Suddenly, there is much talk about the need to erase duplication. The work *downsizing* is being thrown around by secretaries and managers at the water cooler. It is inevitable that some jobs will be lost in the process. Regardless of how important you think you are to a company, companies usually don't need more than one payroll department, one marketing department, or one personnel division. If corporate headquarters in Atlanta or New York has a payroll department, it probably isn't necessary to maintain similar departments at smaller subsidiary operations.

After one company acquires another, the troops come marching in from the home office. Management says it is to help promote an orderly transition, but ultimately, the new troops stay at the expense of the old troops' jobs.

Employees also lose jobs if they do not adjust to the new rules and procedures of the acquiring company. For better or worse, some managers surround themselves with their own crew. They prefer not to keep employees who are still loyal to their old manager or company.

The Layoff.   In the past layoffs happened primarily to people who worked on assembly lines in places like Detroit, Michigan. Not anymore. To survive today, troubled companies are also laying off hundreds of thousands of white-collar employees.

Beware. Management does not always use logic to decide who gets cut from the company team. Seniority helps, but so do competence and office politics.

When Business Is Slow.   When business suddenly drops off, do you think employers are going to be benevolent and keep dozens of unneeded employees on the payroll? No! Witness what happens every year after tourist season. Or look what happens to thousands of accountants after tax season. Or think about the big hirings before Christmas and the big firings after New Year's Day.

Usually, it's nothing personal. It's just reality.

The Most Expendable.   Some more reality. Loyalty is an expensive commodity for corporations. Sometimes, the company values it. Other times, they value it until it starts costing them. That's why, when layoffs are imminent, an employer will often save the newcomers—who get paid substantially less—at the expense of the higher-paid old-timers.

Think of the money that can be saved by replacing a high-paid employee with one or more entry-level employees who work for less.

IS YOUR FIRING IN THE WORKS?

Think you might be in for some trouble?

Bosses have a habit of putting the handwriting right on the wall. Here is how to decode it.

The warning signs:

- You don't get a raise.
- You get a raise, but it stinks.
- The boss starts criticizing your work. A lot.
- You get a bad evaluation. The boss starts putting criticism in writing.
- You notice you are being excluded from meetings.
- Some of your responsibility is taken from you. Your workload is reduced.
- You are moved to a smaller office, or you are told to share your office with another employee.
- You are told to take a special aptitude test that your co-workers don't have to take.
- You find out your boss is checking your credentials. An old boss has been contacted. Your college transcripts have been requested.
- You are given an "assistant" and told to teach him or her everything you know about your job.

GETTING HIT OVER THE HEAD BY A 2 BY 4

Let's take a closer look at three big red flags that suggest your job is at risk:

Money.   If, at review time, you get only a modest raise—or worse, no raise at all—you can either try to find a good excuse or you can recognize what is happening: you have stepped onto the treadmill.

Unless you work for a company that is notoriously cheap or financially ailing, you can expect a cost-of-living raise. If you don't get one, be alert. Your stagnant paycheck is a sign of big trouble.

Evaluations.   Another big sign of trouble is your corporate report card, your evaluation.

The performance evaluation is a management tool that is often used to keep employees in check and in their place. Ideally, it highlights the best of the worker's abilities and makes useful suggestions on how to improve performance.

But the evaluation is also a dissatisfied boss's key documentation in building a case for your dismissal.

Pay attention to everything your boss tells you when she gives you a performance evaluation. It's easy to remember the positive portions of your review and overlook the negative parts.

Read it carefully. Then read it again. If its tone is overtly negative, you *must* take action.

Simply stated, corporate America is impatient. One negative evaluation may be a good attention getter. A second bad evaluation means you are on the hot seat. Rarely can you succeed at a company that gives you two or more consecutive bad reviews.

Over the short run, your boss may notice that your job performance has improved. Should you start making a few mistakes, your boss may believe that you are reverting to the old habits that got you in trouble in the first place.

Warning Notices.   You may get a warning notice after you receive a poor performance review. Warning notices inform you that you're not meeting minimum job requirements and might be terminated shortly.

Large companies are better at giving warning notices than small companies because the larger firms usually have the resources to

Stormy Weather—Negative Performance Evaluations

You never really know if your company considers a bad personnel review sufficient notice for dismissal.

Too many managers give lip service to marginal employees during performance evaluations. They gloss over weaknesses. They send mixed messages. They use subtle criticism. So subtle that employees often don't recognize it to be criticism.

The result? Thousands of unsuspecting people get fired each year.

Watch out when a boss says, "Yes, you can turn your performance around." Hopefully, you can. But what the boss might really mean is: You're not presently working out. You probably won't ever work out. Why don't you start looking for another job?

Here are two examples of performance evaluations for a bank employee. Use them as a guide to determine when it's time to "Get out!"

MEMORANDUM

TO: Personnel file of Donald D. Employee

FROM: Jane R. President

DATE: August 10, 19XX

Donald D. and I recently sat down to review his performance for the first half of the year. This serves as a summary of our discussion.

We discussed the fact that performance in Donald's areas of responsibility has been slipping and that we have had a number of discussions on how to turn around this negative trend. We specifically discussed:

1. Increase in nonperforming assets.
2. Slippage in market share.
3. Lack of proper policies and procedures in Donald's areas of responsibility.
4. Lack of proper follow-up on important problems and issues

such as recent litigation, reorganization of the commercial loan department, and not meeting various deadlines on reports and projects.

5. Lack of business development efforts and community involvement.

Donald and I discussed these problems at length and Donald assured me that these trends would be reversed and the overall performance of his area would improve by year-end. We set specific goals for year-end that are outlined in the corporate performance plan.

I alerted Donald to the serious nature of these performance problems and the urgency in getting these resolved by year-end. I mentioned to him that if the agreed on goals were not met by year-end, we would need to reevaluate his whole area and take additional action that might include a realignment of his responsibilities, restructuring of his area, or similar actions.

Donald indicated he understood the serious nature of current performance problems and assured me that he would meet the goals that we agreed on. During the next six months, I will be closely monitoring Donald's performance and continue follow-up discussions with him.

MEMORANDUM

Personal and confidential

TO: Personnel file of Donald D. Employee

FROM: Jane R. President

DATE: January 26, 19XX

This is a summary of Donald D.'s performance for the second half of 19XX. In conjunction with our joint review of his performance, Donald and I had the following discussion: In November, 19XX, we restructured his management reporting responsibilities; that is, commercial lending now reports to Mike J. instead of Donald. This move came as a result of the poor performance of the commercial lending area and to free up some of Donald's time as deadlines for reports, projects, personnel reviews, and audit responsibilities were not being received in a timely fashion.

To date, these problems have not been eliminated and our discussion centered on a further refinement of responsibilities. While plans have not been finalized, I have asked Donald to think about the following:

1. Restructure Donald's area to include a new group vice president to head up the credit department, processing department, and the management training program.
2. Mike J. would head up the whole corporate banking area and report directly to the president and CEO.
3. Donald would no longer be required to serve on the executive committee.
4. Donald's responsibilities would be realigned to include public relations, community affairs, officer call program, and special projects.

I discussed with Donald that continued poor performance had necessitated these changes. I advised Donald that I was willing to give this a try and hoped that the restructuring would improve his contributions to the company. I made him aware that if there was again no improvement in his performance within the next six months, that he should rethink whether banking is a suitable career in which he can continue to contribute and grow and that he should consider the direction in which his career was headed.

I told him that we would continue to evaluate his effectiveness and contributions during the next six months.

---

wait for someone to quit. (And written warnings are helpful tools to justify a termination if the company is sued for sex, age, or race discrimination.) As a result, few large companies fire employees without written warnings for poor performance on a routine basis. Small companies have limited financial resources; they may fire someone without an official warning notice.

JOB AT RISK? HERE'S WHAT TO DO

Suppose one or more serious warning signs appear on your office horizon. Now what?

Protect yourself. Start looking for a new job.

Act quickly. It is far easier to compete for a job if you already have one. And if you wait too long, it can mean an extended period of unemployment. You may be so hard up for money that you have to settle for a less desirable job.

Even if you turn your situation around, it never hurts to have some irons in the fire. Make sure that you're the one who makes the decision about whether you jump ship or stay.

Here's how to score your next job:

1. Be relentless.
2. Talk to your superior. See the box entitled "There still may be time to save your job."
3. Improve job performance (to buy time or save your job).
4. Check the job market.
5. Get your resume in order.
6. Start networking. Discreetly ask friends and contacts, "Have you heard about any openings?"
7. See employment agencies.
8. Call prospects.
9. Answer ads.
10. Follow up all resumes.
11. Consider starting your own business.
12. Court current clients. Maybe they'll follow.
13. Copy lists, files, and workpapers that you might not have access to once you get fired.
14. Monitor your boss's moods to estimate how much time you have left.

TRAPPED IN THE EYE OF THE STORM: RESIGN OR GET FIRED?

My personal opinion is that smart people have *already* changed jobs. That's if they recognized the warning signs.

TIP

There Still May Be Time to Save Your Job

There still is a chance that you can get a little extra time or another chance to save the job you already have.

"I would go to the boss and say, 'I have a feeling that things aren't going right as far as your view of my performance,'' management recruiter Robert Half said. "I'd like to have a brief talk with you so you can tell me what I can do to straighten it out.''[4]

By communicating your willingness to improve job performance and relationships with co-workers, you may delay an imminent firing.

Being so forthright may have its price. A manager might say, "I'm glad you brought this up'' and proceed to fire you on-the-spot. By taking the initiative, you will either get more time to turn your work situation around or expedite your termination.

But what do you do if you haven't lined up your next job? Are you better off resigning to avoid the so-called stigma of getting fired? Or are you better off choosing the ax?

"If you think you can get a job quickly, it is probably better to quit,'' says management recruiter Robert Half, who founded more than 80 personnel offices that have found positions for more than 100,000 job candidates. But if you can't, remember economics. "You have to support yourself during the period you are unemployed.''[5] You can't collect unemployment benefits if you quit, but you can usually collect them if you're fired.

Relax. Getting fired probably won't affect your ability to get another job. Most employers recognize that someone who resigns without a new job had a few problems, too. If he didn't, he probably wouldn't have quit without lining up a new job. Learn from your mistakes, though.

"The average American will probably have at least seven jobs in his career,'' says Robert Snelling, president of Snelling and Snelling, the world's largest employment service. "Nobody knows if

STRATEGY

Use the Power of Your Current Job to Score the Next One

Use the power of your present job to help you get your next job. Potential employers assume, by default, that you're probably a reasonably good employee if you still work for a company.

You also don't have to worry about a bad reference from your present employer. Your potential employer is usually considerate enough not to check with your current boss for a reference if you ask him not to do so. Just request that your interest in the new company be kept confidential. He will understand that a reference check may jeopardize your employment should your employer find out that you are searching for a new job.

When you change jobs, you can reasonably expect to earn 20 percent more than you did at your last job. As a result, you have to use the implied power of your present position to help you get the best possible salary.

Employers can sense a bargain, and they can hire recently fired employees at fire sale prices. They know that fired employees are often desperate and will work for less because they have mortgage and car payments to make.

anybody got fired anymore. References are practically impossible to check today.''[6] Since companies fear defamation of character lawsuits, most companies will only verify dates of employment and job titles.

WHEN YOU'RE SITTING IN THE HOT SEAT

A virtual library has been written on the subject of employee terminations. Unfortunately, most of it has been written for the benefit of employers to use against their employees. These books explain the mechanics of how to fire someone and make it stick. ''Making it stick'' means building a solid employee dismissal case that will prevail against any future wrongful discharge law suit.

*Looks like they don't want me to come
Monday!*

But little has been said about how an employee can protect himself during a firing.

Most firings start with a boss telling you that he has some bad news for you. He has to let you go. After a conciliatory opening, he explains why he has to terminate you. (Companies that fear litigation might not.)

He then tells you what severance pay and benefits you will receive. He gives you the opportunity to ask any questions that you have about why you're being fired.

Then he ends the meeting. He thanks you for your service to the company. He might say he's sorry things didn't work out.

He tells you to clean out your desk. You give him the key to the front door. He wishes you good luck with your career. You shake hands. Now you're history.

This is the classic textbook firing used by most Fortune 500 and many smaller companies.

STRATEGY

How to Come Out on Top of Your Own Firing

1. Ask for a second chance.
2. Negotiate more severance pay and benefits.
3. Ask your boss for a letter of recommendation.
4. Tell your boss that you want to part as friends.
5. Ask your boss not to discuss your firing with any of your co-workers.

You don't have to follow their protocol for your firing. You should be an active participant and not allow yourself to get trapped by their form firing.

Don't passively sit back and let your firing be dictated by somebody who has the upper hand. After all, this is an important chapter of your life; you are therefore entitled to be the star of your own firing.

You can't afford to get emotional. This is your last chance to transform your textbook firing into a damage control opportunity.

You have to take control of this event. It's your duty to reduce the future ramifications of getting fired while you are actually getting fired.

You need a plan to outmaneuver your boss in order to win a better settlement. As a result, I have developed the following five-step process. Use it to reduce the impact of your firing.

Ask for a Second Chance

Ask, but do not beg, to get your job back. Regardless of how desperate you may be to keep your job, you must maintain your dignity throughout your job's final hour.

Emphasize the positive. Point out to your boss that you're midway through an important project that you would like to finish. Your boss may be unfamiliar with your recent accomplishments and decide to give you additional probationary time. You have absolutely nothing to lose by asking your boss for a second chance. You could gain extra time to start looking for a new job.

If he does not volunteer a little more time, ask for a trial period of one or two months, but be prepared to settle for less.

Negotiate More Severance Pay and Benefits

When your boss discusses severance pay in the initial stage of your firing, remind yourself that it is just an opening bid. You can ask for more money, the right to take some clients if starting your own firm, and health insurance until you get a new job.

Obviously, he doesn't have to accommodate you, but you lose nothing in asking. And do not, under any condition, threaten a wrongful discharge suit against the company if they don't give you what you are asking for. Why? By acting cooperative and assertive, you will probably end up with a better settlement than you were first offered.

Some small companies, with fewer than 20 employees, often cancel health insurance for terminated employees immediately. If you can't get your employer to spring for a couple months of additional coverage, you had better get new coverage immediately. Large companies, with more than 20 employees, are required by federal law to offer you the opportunity to pay for your own continued health insurance.

I stated earlier that you should try to change jobs before you get the ax. Unfortunately, you no longer have that option. So what do you do? If you think you can get a good job quickly, resign. But if you don't have a big nest egg, let your boss fire you so you can file for unemployment benefits.

Be careful. There are more than a few unscrupulous bosses who might coax you to resign. They might say, ''Why don't you resign, instead?'' or ''Resign; you don't want the stigma of getting fired on your resume.'' But what these bosses really mean is, ''Let's keep the company unemployment tax rate low.''

Most companies pay state unemployment tax on their employees. The rate of that costly tax is variable; it's based on the number of former employees who collect unemployment benefits from the state.

Ask Your Boss for a Letter of Recommendation

Probably the last thing most people think about while they are getting fired is their strategy for finding their next job. When you ask your boss for a strong letter of recommendation, you are protecting your ability to get a new job.

When you apply for a new job, a potential employer will check your old references. Why not just hand him a letter from your old boss that details your good points and accomplishments?

Some bosses may say that it is inconsistent to write such a letter for someone they just fired. Nevertheless, try to hold firm. Remind your boss that the letter will help you greatly in finding your next job. Even a letter that describes the dates you worked for the company and the skills you learned on the job can help you get your next job. You probably have some good points that he can list.

Tell Your Boss that You Want to Part As Friends

No matter how angry, devastated, or humiliated you feel, you have to remain dignified throughout your termination party. You may be so furious that the mere thought of being friendly with your worst enemy seems unbearable. However, once you leave the office, you still don't have your next job. At this point, you cannot afford enemies.

You also cannot afford to make a scene. You still need your current boss to give you a reasonably good reference in order to get your next job. Should you part on bad terms, your boss may be reluctant to give you a satisfactory reference.

Now is the time to take the lead and give a monologue similar to the following one:

Let's part as friends. I'm not the type of person who will talk badly about you or the company. Let's part on good terms because this is a small town and we will be traveling in the same circles.

I want to thank you for all the experience I received . . . .

It is natural to feel somewhat hypocritical when you deliver your monologue. But your sole objective is to persuade your boss that you want to part on good terms. If you do this convincingly, your boss may give you a neutral or good recommendation when your next employer calls for a reference.

Ask Your Boss Not to Discuss Your Firing with Any of Your Co-Workers

It can hurt to have a manager with loose lips tell other employees with loose lips damaging things about you. It can hurt even more if all these loose-lipped people spread your private embarrassment around town. Stories about you, whether true or false, can influence your ability to get another job and your professional reputation. You're entitled to privacy.

AFTER IT'S OVER

You are angry and depressed—of course you are. Anyone who tells you not to let it bother you ignores reality. You are human. You have feelings.

What now?

Well, you can mope a little. Give yourself a week. But after that, you have too much to do to wallow in self-pity.

You must keep your self-image high. Do things that make you feel good about yourself. Remind yourself that you are not the only person who has been fired. Think positively—You *will* find a job. You *will* succeed at it. You *will* rise above your troubles.

You're entitled to collect unemployment benefits if you get fired. While the dollar amount of unemployment benefits is probably a fraction of your old salary, it will still come in handy when you want to pay your rent or buy groceries. You can file a claim at your local unemployment compensation office for benefits, which can be as much as 50 percent of your old salary.

If you were to blame for getting fired, *learn from your mistakes.* Make sure you don't repeat them.

And if you weren't responsible? Well, it's usually a waste of time and money to bring a wrongful discharge suit against your former employer. Even if you win, the best you can usually hope for is back pay and your old job.

I think you will be better off if you channel your energy positively into a new job, rather than to spend time and money on a lawsuit that you might not win.

Some people will be unbelievably nosy about your predicament. You don't owe anyone an explanation. That does not mean you can't talk about what happened. Your friends will stand by you.

If someone presses you to divulge why you got fired, keep your answer brief. Say, "Things just didn't work out." Under no circumstances should you say anything that suggests that you are embarrassed or sensitive about getting fired.

Will you be unemployed forever? Of course not. I can't think of a single marketable person who has been unemployed for his entire life. You will have to pound the pavement and hustle a bit, but in the end you will find another job.

A different boss, better working conditions, and friendlier co-workers can often transform a marginal employee into a successful one. You will find a better situation, and you will get back on the fast track.

"It's just like the kid who was the class boob in junior high school who gets a fresh start when his parents move to another state. The kids at the new school don't know what a boob he was at his old school. In a new environment, the kid may thrive and become popular," says Snelling, the employment agency magnate.

"The same can be true when you switch jobs," he says. "At a new job, the new boss may elevate and inspire you. Perhaps you grew up and matured some. You may have changed your way of doing things or modified your desires."[7]

AT A GLANCE

To stay on the fast track, you must:

- Monitor the warning signs that your job is in trouble throughout your career.
- Start looking for another job if serious warning signs appear on your office horizon. You might not be able to salvage your job.
- Be able to support yourself financially while you are unemployed. You can't usually collect unemployment benefits if you resign, but you can if you're fired.
- Realize that you may be fired or laid off at least once during your career. And rise above it.

CHAPTER 8 AUTHOR INTERVIEWS

1. Thomas R. Horton, May 21, 1990.
2. Peter Kurth, June 22, 1988.
3. Marilyn Moats Kennedy, May 16, 1990.
4. Robert Half, June 8, 1988.
5. Ibid.
6. Robert Snelling, May 24, 1988.
7. Ibid.

Chapter Nine

Beating the Stress Mess

"Write all your worries on a sheet of paper," says a workshop instructor to participants at a Fortune 500 Company-sponsored stress management program. "Make a paper airplane out of your sheet. Now, fly it across the room.

"Feel better? All your problems have just disappeared."

Think of all the money you have wasted on similar stress workshops, tapes, and books. And for what? You still feel tense and stressed out.

Psychologists and scientists haven't always taken a sensible approach to the study of stress. "A lot of the work in so-called stress management has been very highly focused and has had no medical basis," says Robert S. Eliot, cardiologist, author of *Is It Worth Dying For?* (Bantam Books) and director of the Institute of Stress Medicine in Denver, Colorado. "It rarely has physiological understanding. And it has been conducted by every profession and non-profession. That is why I think a lot of it hasn't done any good."[1]

Face it. When it comes to stress, you crave answers to these questions: What can you do to prevent stress? How can you stop feeling stressed out? And how can you become more relaxed?

Here's a no-nonsense, program to help you:

1. Prevent stress.
2. Deal with stress.
3. Stay calm in stressful situations.
4. Learn how to relax.

The program works. But you must make a commitment to use it daily. Let's begin.

PART ONE: WARD OFF STRESS

THE RELATIONSHIP BETWEEN WORRY AND STRESS

Did you know cave dwellers had problems dealing with stress, too?

Take Charlie the Caveman, for example. Thousands of years before ESPN, Charlie the Caveman had a rough day in the jungle. He was walking back to his cave when a saber-toothed tiger began to chase him. The beast was hungry and craved a decent meal. (Any one who has tried Slim-Fast knows the feeling.)

Charlie's body reacted to the threat of the tiger by energizing itself. His heart began to beat rapidly. His blood pressure began to rise. Blood rushed into his extremities. His breathing became shallow and rapid. He began to feel, to say the least, anxious.

Charlie had only two options. He could either (1) *fight* the savage beast or (2) *flee*. Regardless of his decision, his body was able to offer extra strength and energy. Physically, Charlie's body was at its maximum efficiency to fight or make a run for it.

Fortunately, in today's world, we no longer have to worry about a saber-toothed tiger attacking us.

Unfortunately, yesterday's caveman has left a frustrating legacy: The fight or flight response. Walter Cannon, a noted physiologist, coined the expression "fight or flight" to help explain why our bodies respond to fear and pressure by producing excess adrenaline and cortisol (*The Wisdom of the Body*, 1939).

As a result, our blood pressure rises, anxiety builds, and we experience other physical changes so that we can deal physically with conflict.

In the 20th century, deadlines, reports, and co-workers do not threaten us the same way the savage beast threatened Charlie the Caveman. Yet we often react to these modern day career challenges with the same powerful physical changes to our bodies that the caveman experienced thousands of years ago.

The legacy of the caveman is that our bodies often operate in a mode better suited to flee a savage beast than to deal with a boss who asks, "Why haven't you finished that project yet?"

LIFE AFTER CHARLIE

What does this mean for you? For starters, how's this: Nearly 50 percent of all heart attacks can't be explained by traditional reasons such as diet, heredity, weight, and smoking.

Doctors Meyer Freidman and Ray H. Rosenman researched this missing link when they wrote about type A and type B personalities in *Type A Behavior and Your Heart* (Knopf). They determined that a substantial portion of the remaining 50 percent of heart attacks was due to stress.

Simply put, the brain puts your body on red alert when it senses a threat to your security. A small gland in your brain, the hypothalmus, signals your pituitary gland to secrete a powerful hormone called ACTH. This hormone stimulates your adrenal glands to release adrenaline.*

Adrenaline is the culprit that causes the heart to pump rapidly, blood pressure to increase, and even more dramatically, to transport blood away from the stomach and skin areas to muscle areas.

---

*Robert S. Eliot and Dennis L. Breo, *Is It Worth Dying For?* (Toronto: Bantam Books, 1984), pp. 27–34.

This is because the muscles will need an extra booster shot of energy.

The body now becomes energized by high-energy fats that are quickly transported into the blood system. Your body is so advanced that it releases chemicals that help blood to clot rapidly in case you are injured. Nerves also stimulate other changes in physiology: Often the muscles of the face become tight, you breathe fast, short breaths, and your blood sugar level increases.

Now your body is ready to offer the strength and endurance that it needs for fight or flight.

But when you react to stress with the fight or flight response, how does it affect your health? During fight or flight, adrenaline and other hormones elevate blood pressure. Over many years, these patterns of elevation can transform temporary increases in blood pressure into permanent increases.

Adrenaline also affects the adhesive abilities of platelets to stick to the walls of your arteries. Once this happens, blood fats can begin to accumulate in these areas. Sadly, your arteries can narrow when these accumulations of fats solidify. Years of bombarding your body with stress chemicals and hormones damage your arteries by leaving places for blood fats to accumulate.

By not taking care of your body and failing to cope with stress, you pave the way for a future heart attack. A fatal heart attack occurs when blood is unable to get through arteries damaged by years of neglect or heredity.

As if heart attacks weren't enough, stress also plays an unsavory role in bringing about hypertension, ulcers, colitis, insomnia, and depression.

THE KEY TO PREVENTING STRESS

Now that you know what the dark side of stress can lead to, are you ready to do something about it? If you said yes, prepare to embark on a two-part stress control program. Part 1 helps you learn how to prevent and reduce stress.

Since some stress is inevitable, your body often reacts physically to it whether you like it or not. Part 2 of the program will show you how to relax your body when this happens.

Just like a buffet dinner where you have a choice between ham and lasagne, you simply choose different relaxation entrees from the stress reduction menu. Pick as many techniques from the menu that you need to satisfy your appetite for less stress and more relaxation.

Here are your entrees: thought control, aerobic exercise, meditation, the stop technique, deep breathing, and progressive muscle relaxation.

It is important to emphasize here that while some techniques offer an immediate antidote for stress, others can take months to master before you achieve the maximum physical and psychological benefits. A technique will only work to the extent that you put the effort into making it work.

Don't be too quick to call it quits if you use a technique once or twice and don't achieve relaxation. You might miss a great way to reduce stress.

Let's explore some strategies that can help you prevent or minimize stress:

1. Monitor your thoughts.
2. Stop worrying about the right problem at the wrong time.
3. Just say "Stop"!
4. Accept blame and do something about your problems.
5. Be realistic about your expectations of life.
6. Get organized!

MONITOR AND CONTROL YOUR THOUGHTS

Whether you recognize it or not, the single best way to prevent stress in your life is to modify and combat your negative thoughts.

If you can, try to listen to all the negative thoughts that you tell yourself each day. Write a check mark on a notepad whenever you find yourself thinking a negative thought. At the end of the day, you'll probably be amazed by the number of check marks you've written.

Think of it: Each check mark represents one thought that played a significant role in the amount of stress that you experienced that day.

This is where modifying and combating your negative thoughts fits in. Richard A. White, a psychotherapist and lecturer, told me:

I really believe that 90 percent of the stress that people go through in this life is created by the thoughts that people have. It is not a bad boss. It is not an overload of paperwork. It is not a deadline.

All those thoughts are floating around, but I think the creation of stress is the thoughts that go along with it: I can't meet this deadline. I've got a terrible boss. Why is my boss always picking on me? I hate this job. My co-workers are all S.O.B.s. Why am I stuck in this job? I don't earn enough money.

Pick a thought. All these thoughts initiate negative feelings and emotions which lead to frustration, anger, worry, depression, and anxiety.

Out of that whole rush of catastrophic thinking, a whole stream of negative feelings is going to come from those thoughts. To the extent that you feel these things, a chemical reaction (fight or flight) begins to start pumping into your system.[2]

Let's take a closer look at how thoughts create stress with the following examples.

The thoughts of an employee who notices that his boss winked at him in a strange way:

- *Negative approach:* "He must be upset with me." "I probably should have put a lot more effort into the report I gave him." "He probably hates the report." "Maybe he is thinking about firing me."
- *Positive approach:* "Maybe the boss has a contact lens problem." "Maybe he got something in his eye." "I'm going to focus my attention on my work."[3]

The thoughts of an accountant with a deadline:

- *Negative approach:* "If I don't get this tax return finished by 4 P.M., my boss is going to be very upset with me. Then he'll give me a lousy review. I bet we lose the client."
- *Positive approach:* "I know I can get this done by tomorrow." "Maybe I'll ask the boss if I can have some extra time." "I'll work an hour later tonight."

The thoughts of an applicant during a job interview:

- *Negative approach:* "How dare he ask me that question!" "Why is he making me feel so frustrated?" "I bet I don't get this job." "He has no right to make me feel nervous."
- *Positive approach:* "I feel happy." "I feel confident." "It is a beautiful day." "The sun is shining." "I hope I get this job." "He looks interested in what I'm saying."

These examples show that most predicaments are, for the most part, neutral experiences. The mere act of a manager blinking an eye is not a positive or negative experience. Neither is a deadline or a job interview. Each of these situations is identical. The only thing that changed was the person's mental outlook toward the circumstances.

You usually have a choice to interpret conflicts either positively or negatively. The only thing that is positive or negative is how you allow your thoughts to react to an experience.

"The key to stress prevention is to take a look at your thoughts and eliminate thoughts that produce stress for you and put different nonstress-producing thoughts in their place," says psychotherapist White.[4]

Learn to listen to your thoughts. That little voice inside your head can be your best friend or your worst enemy. To prevent stress, learn how to make that little voice be your best friend.

That's why you have to pay attention to negative thoughts before they create feelings of stress or pressure. When you catch yourself thinking a negative thought, say, "Wait a minute! That is a negative thought . . . but that isn't really true."

What's more, you may have to tell yourself positive thoughts 500 or more times a day to counteract negative thoughts such as: "I shouldn't have said that." "I made a big mistake." "I should have kept my mouth shut about that." "I was a fool to speak up during that staff meeting."

Take heed: Monitor and change your negative thoughts before they make you feel stressed out.

STOP WORRYING ABOUT THE RIGHT PROBLEM AT THE WRONG TIME

Your subconscious mind, the part you are not aware of, often sends distracting thoughts into your consciousness. These thoughts interrupt your concentration from the task at hand. Around the office, these thoughts can interfere with job performance and cause added stress. At home, they can hinder you from fully enjoying many pleasant experiences.

Consider the following example:

Andrea thinking to herself at work, Tuesday 2:25 P.M.:

I wonder if Terry is still mad at me. Maybe I shouldn't have acted so abruptly last night. Anyway, I can't wait until we go skiing in Colorado. . . . Maybe I should buy some new ski boots for the trip? I probably shouldn't waste money on boots. . . . Perhaps the red ones in the window at Champs would do the trick. But, they are so expensive. . . . Oh, what the hell, what's MasterCard for, anyway?

Andrea thinking to herself at the Copper Mountain Ski Resort the following Saturday at 7 P.M.:

I don't know how I can possibly finish the Robins account presentation by Wednesday afternoon. I don't like how the mock print advertisement turned out. Maybe I should have made the color emphasis less bold and more subtle?

Is it too late to change print copy? I wonder if I can get a decent photographer? What if Mr. Robins loathes my presentation? If that happens, God, I hope I won't lose my job.

Mr. Robins didn't seem very receptive to my ideas during the initial conference. On the other hand, maybe he was pretending to be apathetic?

No doubt about it, worry is a necessary part of human problem solving. Actually, everything that Andrea is worrying about are problems that she should be worrying about.

Yet Andrea is not worrying efficiently. For the most part, there was very little Andrea could do at the ski lodge in Colorado that could influence how Mr. Robins would respond to a presentation on Wednesday.

Andrea is guilty of worrying about the right problem at the wrong time. The result? Andrea does not fully enjoy her ski weekend. Instead of enjoying the skiing and scenery, Andrea is thinking about Mr. Robins and the possibility of losing her job.

When she returns from her ski trip, Andrea's aimless worrying may lead to additional stress and poor job performance. She may have to work a stressful marathon shift to repair the Robins account. By devoting extra attention to this account, she might cause even more trouble for herself if she can't complete her other projects on time.

Andrea is not alone. Many people also allow their worries to interfere with their job performance and the ability to enjoy their home life. If you don't worry efficiently, you can use the Stop technique to focus your attention from a troublesome thought back to the task at hand.

JUST SAY "STOP!"

Whenever you start worrying about the right problem at the wrong time, *silently* shout the word *stop*.

At work, Andrea should have said *stop* the minute she started thinking about the ski trip. This would have redirected her concentration to work rather than her personal problems.

Similarly, if she started worrying about her career problems during her vacation, she should have told herself *stop*. This would have helped her to enjoy her weekend ski trip with Terry.

The Stop technique is the grandfather of many modern day stress prevention techniques. Although some stress educators now prefer other cognitive thinking approaches, the Stop technique is nonetheless a powerful tool that many people use to control stress.

You may get more mileage from the Stop technique than other thought substitution techniques. The technique can help take your mind off distracting thoughts instantly.

If you like the Stop technique, use it as many times as necessary to help you concentrate. Some people use the technique more than 100 times each day.

ACCEPT BLAME AND DO SOMETHING ABOUT YOUR PROBLEMS

Suppose you were bypassed for a promotion you were promised and felt you deserved. It would be natural for you to be upset about this common office injustice for a few weeks, but it would be self-destructive to be angry and bitter three months later.

Don't allow your thoughts to dwell on what a horrible boss or job you have. Instead, channel the anger inside you positively toward a new goal.

Perhaps your positive attitude may keep you in the running for the next promotion. Maybe you'll find a dream job at some other company. Who knows? You may even go into business for yourself.

Of course, I know it's incredibly easy to blame another person for your problems. But one thing is for sure—you're not lobbying for the next promotion, typing resumes, or investigating business opportunities when you allow disappointment to fester.

Successful people usually have something in common: They are comfortable with responsibility.

We envy these people and wonder: Did they get all the lucky breaks in the world? Was success handed to them on a silver plat-

> *The Serenity Prayer of Alcoholics Anonymous*
>
> God grant me the serenity to accept the things I cannot change, the courage to change the things I can, and the wisdom to know the difference.

ter? Was the path to success easy? The answer to all these questions is an emphatic *no!*

Do successful people work hard for their success? Yes. Do they accept responsibility for their own actions? Yes. Do they have a healthy self-esteem? Yes. Do they believe in themselves and their own abilities? You bet your Reeboks!

You too can cross the threshold of success. Just accept responsibility for your own actions.

A good way to do this is to learn a beautiful prayer called the Serenity Prayer. It's used in Alcoholics Anonymous recovery programs in the United States.

It isn't known for sure who wrote the Serenity Prayer. According to Alcoholics Anonymous, the prayer is usually attributed to Reinhold Niebuhr, a 20th-century theologian. The reason the prayer's true author isn't known for certain is because Niebuhr credited theologian Friedrich Oetinger with writing it.

For our discussion purposes, it doesn't matter if Niebuhr or Oetinger wrote the Serenity Prayer. What matters is that the prayer illustrates how to stop blaming others for problems and start accepting responsibility for actions.

BE REALISTIC ABOUT YOUR EXPECTATIONS OF LIFE

"Nothing is impossible!" "You can do anything you set your mind on!" "The sky's the limit." During my many years with the Jaycees, I've heard many motivational speakers express these inspirational themes. Yet I feel these highly persuasive speakers aren't entirely truthful when they deliver these impassioned messages to audiences across the country.

In the real world, some things are impossible. You can't always do everything you set your mind to. And "The sky's the limit" is nothing but an old cliche. Face it, not every person has what it takes to be a neurosurgeon or a bank president.

You must remember to add the clause "within the framework of your human ability" whenever you hear a motivational speaker say remarks like, "You can do anything you set your mind on." You should also view similar messages expressed in books and other media within the same context. Always look at overly optimistic quotes such as "If you think you can, you can—If you think you can't, you are right," within the framework of your human ability.

Don't misunderstand me. In no way am I saying that you have to cop out and set safe, comfortable goals for yourself. Hardly.

Throughout life, always push yourself to the outer limits of what you are capable of doing. Match yourself against the biggest challenge you can find that stimulates personal growth and expands your horizon.

There is nothing wrong with failing to reach a worthwhile goal. But don't set yourself up for an exercise in futility because you saddle yourself with totally unrealistic expectations.

Try to set goals for yourself that are within your control. Instead of saying, "I'm going to get a job with the *New York Times*," say "I'm going to be the best writer that I can be." You can control how well you write, but you can't control a hiring decision made by the *New York Times*.

When you set realistic goals, you'll probably find you have less stress. You may also gain self-esteem and self-confidence because you are succeeding, not struggling.

GET ORGANIZED!

Wise up! Handle job stress before it handles you.

Here's how to cut down on job stress:

Do Your Most Important Tasks First.   Rank everything you want to accomplish each day on a list. It's also a good idea to plan a time budget that details how much time you should spend with each item. Strive to complete your high-priority tasks first. Once you finish them, you can move on to lower priority tasks.

Don't Bite Off More than You Can Chew.   Use the word *no* more often in your life. If your workload is at maximum capacity, don't do a task for a co-worker if it will cause you to fall behind at your own job responsibilities. However, if no one else is available, don't turn down a project that your boss considers to be urgent. Ask her to help you prioritize the new assignment in light of your present responsibilities.

Eliminate Unnecessary Interruptions.   Try to manage daily work interruptions. If you're successful, you can gain extra time to finish other job duties.
Here's how:

- Make telephone calls more productive; outline what you plan to discuss and group calls together.
- If necessary, use a secretary or answering machine to screen telephone calls.
- Schedule appointments and sales calls for a certain day.
- Reschedule meetings if you feel pressed.
- Leave time in your schedule for drop-in visitors and rush jobs.
- If you need to get some serious work done, put a sign on your door that says "Quiet hour." (Beware: this strategy often annoys bosses and co-workers.)

Make Yourself Decisive.   You can waste a lot of energy if you prolong making decisions. Always give yourself a time limit to make a decision. But don't go for the overkill, drown in minutiae. Remember, most decisions can be made if you have the main facts.

Once you make a decision, stop worrying about it. Don't continue to second guess yourself by saying, ''Maybe I should have

*Buried by paperwork? Work at getting
more organized.*

. . . I think I made a mistake . . . On the other hand . . . I was right
the first time.''

Don't Get Buried by Paperwork.   Keep your desktop and work
space clean and uncluttered; you won't have to waste much time
looking for ink pens and files.

Don't waste time trying for absolutely perfect written correspondence if it's not necessary. If your message is concise and understandable, don't keep revising it.

You might also realize a big timesaving if you learn how to do
your own word processing. (Typing is for everyone, not just secretaries.)

Read the Important Stuff.   Learn how to read faster and increase your reading comprehension. Don't waste time reading all
the junk mail that is delivered to your office. Make an effort to read
information that is relevant to your job or profession.

Don't burden yourself by reading every single word in professional journals. Often, you can read such journals the same way
you would read a newspaper. Keep abreast of professional developments by reading the headlines and significant items in depth. If

you need more detailed information later, you'll know where to look.

PART TWO: HOW TO MANAGE STRESS AND ACHIEVE RELAXATION

By now, it may have occurred to you that the first part of your stress management program emphasizes getting a grip on thoughts before your body turns on its fight or flight mode.

Yet, there are times in life when you *will* have a physical response to stress. When this happens, here are some surefire methods to relax:

1. Working out.
2. Meditation.
3. Progressive muscle relaxation.

WORKING OUT

"There are times I've been angry enough to tell off bank customers, but I keep quiet," says Kim, a management trainee. "Instead of telling a customer off, I jog and lift weights at a fitness center after work. This allows me to keep my job and work out my frustration."

"There is a lot of research that suggests that exercise reduces feelings of anxiety, physical tiredness, and depression," says Dr. David Emorling, executive director of the National Wellness Institute.[5]

When you build greater physical stamina, your body improves its physical reaction to stress. Your added self-confidence, which comes from knowing that you are in shape, may also give you a competitive edge.

That edge may help you to feel that you are better equipped mentally to deal with difficult conflicts. At times when others are exhausted or burned out, you may have the stamina to endure extra stress.

Sound incredible? Here's some more proof. Dr. Robert S. Brown, a psychiatrist and medical researcher at the University of Virginia, has a database of 10,000 subjects who reduced stress and enhanced their mental well-being by adopting an exercise program.[6]

Each semester, students in Brown's mental health course have a choice between writing a lengthy term paper or exercising three times a week for a minimum of 20 to 30 minutes. Since students usually have a dislike for term papers, most opt to jog, swim, walk, or play tennis.

At the beginning of the one-semester course, students are given standard psychological tests and are also tested to see how far they can run and how many push-ups and sit-ups they can do. Weight, height, and blood pressure readings are also recorded for students.

For the rest of the semester, students record their mood before exercise, during exercise, and after exercise on a scale of 1–10 in a pocket exercise journal they carry with them. Students also record an estimate of how long it took them to reach their peak mood after each workout.

At the end of the course, testing and measurements are repeated for comparison. "I have found that those students who become physically fit will have significant improvement in all tests of psychological functioning including decreased levels of anxiety, decreased levels of depression, increased levels of cheerfulness, decreased anger and hostility. And, maybe even improved short-term memory," said Dr. Brown.[7]

So remember, aerobic exercise can be a good way to work out stress and manage problems (not to mention a good way to avoid a term paper at the University of Virginia).

FORGET THE GURU STEREOTYPE— WHITE–COLLAR WORKERS MEDITATE, TOO

We live in a country where more than 9 million people are alcohol dependents;* nearly 6 million people are alcohol abusers.† More

---

*NIAAA and the U.S. Bureau of the Census, Series P–25, No.1018–1/89, "Epidemiological Bulletin 23" Alcohol, Health and Research World (vol. 13, no. 4), p. 368.
†NIAAA and the U.S. Bureau of the Census, "Epidemiological Bulletin 23" Alcohol, Health and Research World (vol. 13, no. 4), p. 368.

than 1 million people used Valium and other powerful tranquilizers a month;* heart disease claims hundreds of thousands of lives each year. And more than one out of every five people has high blood pressure.†

Also, millions of Americans are overweight, smoke cigarettes, and suffer from depression.

Armed with this knowledge, you can see that anyone who thinks you are slightly weird because you meditate to cope with stress is mistaken.

There are many Americanized versions of meditation that are void of religious implication, incense, and strange music. All versions help you to rid your body of stress and spur relaxation. Surprisingly, the techniques are easy to master. And many people claim 15 minutes of meditation provides them with the same relaxation and therapeutic benefits as an hour-and-a-half nap.

The only problem with meditation is that there are times and places where you feel stressed out and just can't meditate. Obviously, if you share an office with 20 people, you can't get up and leave your work space. Still, you can use meditation to relax when you come home from the office.

Meditation takes practice. The more you practice, the better the results. You'll probably feel less agitated, more calm, and less high-strung. And troubling thoughts won't bother you as much when you realign your thought process.

Use the following technique once or twice a day for best results. Don't worry if you miss meditating for a day or two. The important thing is to incorporate meditation into your pattern of living and make it a valuable part of your life.

Try to wait two hours after eating a meal before you start meditating; your digestive system may interfere with your efforts to achieve relaxation immediately after eating.

---

*National Institute on Drug Abuse statistics from their 1988 national household survey; confirmed December 11, 1990 by Samantha Helfert, an information specialist with The National Clearing House for Alcohol and Drug Information.
†John Berkow, ed., *The Merck Manual of Diagnosis and Therapy* (Rahway: Merck, Sharp, and Dome Research Laboratories, 1987), p. 392.

TACTIC

A Simple Way to Meditate*

1. Try to find a quiet room without distractions such as telephones, stereos, or other people.
2. Sit in a comfortable chair in an upright position.
3. Shut your eyes.
4. Try to relax your muscles. Start by relaxing the muscles of your feet and gradually work your way up to the muscles of your head.
5. Take five deep abdominal breaths.
6. Visualize a serene pond in a hilly countryside on a summer day. View your thought process as a mountain pond. An air bubble comes to the surface of the pond whenever you have a different thought. Another thought, another air bubble comes to the surface.

    With meditation you want to concentrate on pleasant comforting thoughts, not thoughts that make you anxious or nervous. Pleasant thoughts might be, "Drinking a Pina Colada on a white sandy beach," or "That was a good TV show I saw last night." Unpleasant thoughts would be, "How am I going to pay my mortgage this month?" or, "I can't believe the paltry salary increase I received."

    Get the big picture? You constantly bombard yourself with negative thoughts each day. That's why you need to realign your thought process to stop worrying and start relaxing.

    When you meditate, always visualize the tranquil pond and air bubbles. Your mission is to make your mind resemble the tranquil pond with a calm, flat surface, without any air bubbles.

7. Whenever you have a negative air bubble thought such as, "My boss was upset with me today," you need to redirect your attention positively. You do this by saying your own one-

---

*Adapted from Herbert Benson and Miriam Z. Klipper, *The Relaxation Response* (New York: Avon Books, 1976), pp. 160–65.

syllable word to overcome distracting thoughts, then breathing in and out through your nose.

Choose a one-syllable word. Some examples: *ohm, one, own,* and so on. After you exhale, say your one-syllable word to yourself. For example, say, "one." Now breathe in . . . out, "one." Breathe in . . . out, "one." Do this until the negative thought and air bubble evaporates.

Repeat your defense word until your stress-provoking thought has disappeared. Your word is a shield to use against the stress-producing thoughts that may cause you to worry.

8. Meditate for 10 to 25 minutes. (Worried about meditating too long? No problem! Just open your eyes to check the time.)

Your goal is to clean out the cobwebs of excess worry from your brain. You will start to feel more relaxed. Eventually, you won't have to concentrate on pleasant thoughts because you will know how to realign your thoughts.

9. When you are through, count backward from 10 to 5. Then say: Five, you will be relaxed; four, you will be refreshed; three, you will be alert; two, you will be aware; on the count of one, open your eyes, you are wide awake; one, you are wide awake.

When you come home at the end of a tough day, use meditation to help you forget the office and enjoy your family life. Of course, you may have to postpone your meditation until after dinner when the children are asleep.

RELAX YOUR MUSCLES

Deep muscle relaxation helps you to recognize the early warning signs of stress. This allows you to induce relaxation by tensing and then relaxing various muscle groups. Besides achieving a relaxed state, deep muscle relaxation also has a positive energizing effect.

While you can teach yourself these exercises, there are many relaxation tapes on the market that walk you through the process.

Tapes can be purchased from physicians, stress counselors, and health-oriented bookstores.

Many progressive muscle relaxation tapes consist of a soothing voice that guides you through a process to tense and relax various muscles. For example, a relaxation tape might say:

Focus on the muscles in your feet. Now point your toes toward your head to tense the muscles in your feet and legs. Press your toes away from the head and point them toward the floor. Feel the tension. Notice how the tension is tight and uncomfortable. Hold the tension in your ankles for five seconds. Now let the muscles of your feet relax completely.

The tape then guides you step-by-step to tense and relax the muscles of your lower legs, thighs, abdomen, shoulders, forehead and face, arms, and hands.

Some tapes emphasize visualization rather than progressive muscle relaxation. They are designed to transport you via your imagination to places such as a beautiful mountain or a beach in an exotic land. A relaxation tape that uses imagery rather than muscle exercises to achieve relaxation may say, ''You are on a beach in Tahiti. Feel that tropical sunshine beating down on your skin. Smell the scent of the coconut in the air. Hear the waves beat on the shore. See the waves roll in and out.''

After you have listened to a tape, you'll probably feel relaxed and refreshed. With practice, many people often learn to induce the same physical and mental relaxation without using relaxation tapes.

AT A GLANCE

Stress is one adversary that you have to fight on two fronts. First, try to prevent a physical reaction to stress. To do this:

1. Monitor and control your thoughts.
2. Use the stop technique.
3. Stop worrying about the right problem at the wrong time.
4. Set realistic goals.

5. Accept responsibility for your problems.
6. Get organized at work.

Second, your body often reacts physically to stress, whether you like it or not. When this happens, try to bring about relaxation with:

1. Exercise.
2. Meditation.
3. Relaxation tapes.

CHAPTER 9 AUTHOR INTERVIEWS

1. Robert S. Eliot, August 9, 1988.
2. Richard A. White, May 12, 1988.
3. Ibid.
4. Ibid.
5. David Emorling, June 1, 1990.
6. Robert S. Brown, June 1, 1990.
7. Ibid.

Chapter Ten
Coming on Strong

Cliff Lothery, former associate director for Program Services and Health Enhancement for the U.S. YMCA, once said, "I think society and the world can look at decisions that were made by influential people, in major meetings, and under stressful conditions. There are a lot of decisions made in government, religion, politics, and industry by people who are so fatigued and relatively unhealthy that they would not have made those decisions if they were stronger or healthier.

"A lot of people say, 'I'm not strong enough or healthy enough. I don't have enough vim and vigor to go that extra mile.' "[1]

NOTE: Any and all directions, instructions, and suggestions contained in this book regarding physical, manual, or mental exercises, procedures, and/or directions and all health care recommendations are described solely for informational purposes. Medical information in this chapter was reviewed for medical accuracy by R. Whit Curry, Jr., MD, Interim Chairman, Department of Community Health and Family Medicine, University of Florida College of Medicine. The author and publisher specifically disclaim any and all liability for the reader's injury, damage, or loss due to or relating in any way to the use of any and all exercises, procedures, and health care recommendations. Author and publisher recommend that the reader seek proper medical advice from a physician prior to initiating any physical exercise or procedure, or undertaking any health care recommendation.

He's right. Good health plays a major role in your career effectiveness. And eating too many meals of pizza and beer, being overweight, or smoking cigarettes could cause *you* to fizzle out of the
career game.

- Perhaps you're 41, but look 54. You work 60-hour weeks,
  smoke two packs a day, and have packed more than a few
  pounds on your frame since college. This chapter is for you.
- Maybe you're 39 and have already had 10 jobs, but you still
  ache for a high-paying job with a corner office. This chapter
  is for you.
- Perhaps you're 29, and your career is pure fast track. You
  don't smoke. You watch your nutrition and work out at a
  gym three times a week. This chapter is for you, too.

You might wonder why I included a wellness chapter in *How to
Make Your Boss Work for You*. Well, it's because I'm a *big* believer in
preventive medicine. What good is that corner office if you die prematurely from a heart attack, stroke, or lung cancer?

By the same token, you may not have found all the success you
wanted yet. A healthy lifestyle, on average, may enable you to
have a longer, more productive career. You may be a late bloomer,
after all.

And if you already use a program of preventive medicine? Keep
up the good work. Use this chapter as a refresher.

You *must* safeguard your future productivity and health. Aside
from departures due to the fickle finger of fate, healthy people usually don't get ejected from the career game prematurely.

"Over the next 30 years, someone who is now in their early 30s,
10 percent overweight, smokes, and has a high-stress job, increases his risk for heart disease or cancer four to five times the national average," says Dr. David Emorling of the National Wellness
Institute.[2]

Before I go any further, let me define the term *wellness*. According to the National Wellness Institute, wellness is an active process
of becoming aware of and making choices toward a more successful existence. It's a process that a person does daily. You do this
step by step to promote a healthy lifestyle.[3]

A striking feature of your individual advancement program is wellness. In this chapter, you'll learn eight nutrition and fitness rules to build health, energy, and stamina for a long, productive career.

The Eight Rules of Wellness

1. Don't let your arteries look like jelly doughnuts.
2. Stop smoking.
3. Control caffeine consumption.
4. Don't use alcohol to cope with stress.
5. Beware of the silent killer.
6. Get enough sleep.
7. Exercise.
8. Wear safety belts.

DON'T LET YOUR ARTERIES LOOK LIKE JELLY DOUGHNUTS

You've heard the news reports. You know a diet high in cholesterol and saturated fats is bad news. Still, you probably haven't changed your diet much.

Why? Well, news reports are often difficult to understand; they talk in highly technical terms. And they're not very exciting to read, either.

Take the Surgeon General's Report on Nutrition and Health,* for example. It reveals that diet plays a significant role each year in:

- Heart disease, which kills more than 760,000 people.
- Cancer, which kills more than 470,000 people.
- Strokes, which kill nearly 150,000 people.

Pretty scary statistics. Unfortunately, most people don't relate well to health statistics. Numbers seem far removed from their

---

*United States Office of the Assistant Secretary for Health, *The Surgeon General's Report on Nutrition and Health* (Washington, D.C.: U.S. Government, 1988) pp. 1–720.

everyday life, and there's always something more pressing to think about.

It just isn't enough to know that thousands of people die from dread diseases each year. Most people prefer to put their fears on the back burner. They delude themselves into believing that it—the Big C, the heart attack—will never happen to them.

These people won't change their nutrition habits until they genuinely believe that yes, it could happen to them. They need to realize that while genetic predisposition is an inherent part of these diseases, thousands of deaths could have been prevented with a healthier diet. And one of those thousands could be yours.

Accordingly, I've written this section to help explain the likely consequences of eating too many breakfasts of bacon and eggs and too many steak dinners.

Picture a plain doughnut and a jelly doughnut. Except for size, a cross-section of an artery of a child or a teenager has the same shape of a plain doughnut, with a large doughnut hole.

When you eat foods high in saturated fats, such as fatty meats and dairy products, you increase the rate that your body makes unhealthy LDL cholesterol (LDL means low-density lipoprotein). Cholesterol is a fatty, waxlike substance that is the principal ingredient of plaque. The liver produces all the cholesterol that your body needs.

Your liver then packages fat and cholesterol into packets called lipoproteins and sends them into your blood stream. The fat in these packages is called on to create energy or is stored for later use. The lipoproteins then nourish other cells with needed cholesterol. After the cells have been nourished, excess cholesterol from low-density lipoproteins is deposited along the walls of your arteries.

After years of dietary neglect, these deposits accumulate and make it difficult for blood to flow through an artery. In other words, after years of eating the wrong food, a cross-section of your artery now looks like a jelly doughnut with a very small hole instead of a plain doughnut with a nice navigable hole. A heart attack occurs when blood is unable to get through a clogged coronary artery. Similarly, strokes take place when an artery carrying blood to the brain is blocked.

Nearly 760,000 men and women will die because of heart disease this year.* Many of these people would be alive today if they had changed their diet to one low in fat and cholesterol. While there is not a conclusive link between a diet high in saturated fat and heart disease, there is strong evidence that suggests that both are highly correlated (1984 Coronary Primary Prevention Trials).

The National Cholesterol Education Program of the Heart, Lung and Blood Institute has established standards to help you monitor the level of cholesterol in your body. According to the Institute, the typical American needs to reduce his daily consumption of fat by approximately 10 percent. Today most Americans eat a diet that contains roughly 40 percent fat each day. But the Heart, Lung and Blood Institute believes that a healthy diet should average 30 percent or less for calories from fat and have no more than 10 percent saturated fat.†

The American Heart Association recommends a daily intake of less than 300 milligrams of cholesterol a day.‡ If you eat one egg yolk a day, 213 milligrams of cholesterol, you've practically met your entire cholesterol intake for that day.

They also recommend that a physician test the level of cholesterol in your blood on a regular basis. Test results show whether the level of cholesterol is desirable, borderline acceptable, or if you have a high risk for heart disease.

Test results are usually measured in milligrams per deciliter. Generally, a test result of less than 200 is considered to be within a healthy or desirable range. However, a test result that is between 200–239 for adults 20 and over strongly suggests that you should change your diet. If you haven't reduced your diet to a cholesterol level of less than 300 milligrams a day, you should do so.

If your test score is above 240, you have a high risk for heart disease. This means that you should make major changes in your diet

---

*The Surgeon General's Report on Nutrition and Health, pp. 1–720.

†The National Cholesterol Education Program of the National Heart, Lung and Blood Institute, *The Report of the Expert Panel of Population, Strategies for Blood Cholesterol Reduction* (Bethesda, MD: NHLBI, November 1990), pp. 17–23.

‡American Heart Association, *Cholesterol and Your Heart* (Dallas: American Heart Association, 1989), p.10.

by reducing your consumption of fat and cholesterol. If dietary changes don't bring the level of cholesterol in your blood to a healthy level, your physician will probably prescribe a special medication and recommend even more changes in your diet.

Dr. Charles B. Arnold, Jr., medical director of Metropolitan Life Insurance Company, believes that most adults need a diet that is low in saturated fat and cholesterol. Dr. Arnold told me:

> In the United States today, the average cholesterol level is about 215 milligrams per deciliter. It probably should be under 200.
>
> Average daily intake for adults should not exceed 300 milligrams of cholesterol daily.
>
> One should probably strive to get one's cholesterol down below 200. Not everyone can do that. But with a physician's and nutritionist's help, it is certainly possible for the average person to reduce blood cholesterol at least 10 percent lower than it is today—regardless of that level.[4]

Always remember that plaque continues to deposit along the walls of your arteries throughout your life.

"We know that cholesterol tends to rise with age in Americans," says Dr. Thomas Kottke, a cardiologist and preventive medicine specialist at the Mayo Clinic. "If you are a 25-year-old businessman and your cholesterol level is 195, that's high for 25 years old.

"That means by the time you are 50 years old you will probably be around 250. That's definitely high and puts you at fairly high risk for a heart attack," says Dr. Kottke.[5]

In other words, if you test normal today, it does not mean that you can eat all the fatty food you want to with no worry about tomorrow. To do so invites a cholesterol test score in future years that may be rated borderline or at high risk for heart disease.

Some corporate climbers are under the erroneous impression that a healthy diet means a vegetarian diet. T'aint necessarily so. You can probably still eat a juicy T-Bone steak, ice cream, or doughnuts. Just eat them in moderation. (Check with your doctor to determine what is appropriate for you.)

Here are some tips from the American Heart Association* and the National Heart, Lung and Blood Institute† for a healthy diet:

- Try to eat red meat (beef, pork, or lamb, which are high in fat and cholesterol) no more than one or two days a week.
- Don't go overboard on the days you eat fatty meats—try to keep your servings at about six ounces. Eat less regular hamburger, bacon, hot dogs, sausage, luncheon meats, and other fatty or red meats.
- Trim the excess fat off meat and use lean cuts.
- Eat egg yolks only in moderation. Try to eat no more than three a week. (Remember, eggs are found in many non-breakfast foods such as cakes and breads.)
- Eat more fish and poultry—they are usually much lower in fat and cholesterol than red meat.
- Remove the skin and excess fat when you eat poultry.
- Reduce your consumption of foods loaded with oils that contain saturated fat for flavoring or preservative purposes. Coconut and palm oil are prime examples of oils that fall into this category.
- How you cook food affects the amount of fat and cholesterol you consume each day. It is usually better to broil, roast, bake, or microwave food instead of frying it (sorry, Butter Flavor Crisco fans!).
- Use some of the new low-fat dairy products instead of traditional dairy products with higher fat and cholesterol levels. Skim milk is a healthy substitute for whole milk, and there are many cheese products that come in low-fat and reduced calorie varieties. Egg Beaters is a tasty egg product that has most of its cholesterol removed. If you have a sweet tooth, substitute low-fat yogurt or ice milk for ice cream.

---

*American Heart Association, *Cholesterol and Your Heart,* p. 11–19.
†The National Cholesterol Education Program of the National Heart, Lung and Blood Institute, pp. 17–23.

- Since butter is full of cholesterol, use margarine as a substitute to flavor your food. (Some companies now offer low-fat, no-cholesterol, and low-salt margarines.)
- While salads and greens are quite healthy, salad dressing and oils can be a big culprit in the diet game. Good news: Mayonnaise and mayonnaise substitutes come in low-fat, low-salt, and reduced calorie varieties. (Beware: Load up a salad with regular dressing, real bacon bits, and other goodies, and you may create a salad with more fat and calories than a Big Mac and french fries.)
- Increase your consumption of whole-grain and fiber products. Fiber-filled breads and cereals are a source of protein. They also have many health benefits that range from reducing cholesterol levels and to preventing cancer of the colon.
- Fruits, vegetables, grains, and legumes are usually low in fat and have no cholesterol. Many are good low calorie snacks.
- Cut down on bakery goods. They're loaded with calories and are often made with egg yolks and saturated fats.

Body Weight Management and Salt

Weight Management. "We are fat. We are a nation that has gone from living off the fat of the land to becoming the fat of the land," says Dr. Thomas Kottke of the Mayo Clinic.[6]

While how to lose weight is beyond the scope of this book, the importance of maintaining a lean body weight is not.

From a physical point of view, any extra pounds on your frame force your heart and circulatory system to work much harder. Over the years, obesity (meaning more than 20 percent above ideal body weight) can contribute to a disastrous assortment of unpleasant health problems. "Weight is associated with several chronic illnesses such as diabetes and high blood pressure," says Dr. James Marx of the Centers for Disease Control."[7]

From a psychological point of view, many people are less able to function socially or at work if they feel self-conscious about being overweight. And in some jobs, having an attractive, trim presence may be essential. Thus, if you really want to be healthy, lose those extra pounds!

Salt. For many people there is a link between salt (sodium chloride) intake and high blood pressure. Cutting excess salt from your diet may help you avoid high blood pressure or help normalize your blood pressure. The average American eats 12 to 36 times the salt the body requires each day.*

Why? What confuses many people are foods that have plenty of salt in them before they even shake the salt shaker. That's because the preservatives in food are often loaded with sodium.

Resist the temptation to shake that salt shaker to flavor food unless it's absolutely necessary. Try to avoid salty foods such as potato chips, pretzels, salted peanuts, soy sauce, and cured meats. There are salt substitutes that taste similar to salt without having its negative health aspects.

SMOKERS: AVOID READING THIS SECTION AT YOUR OWN RISK

Sigh! Not another smoking lecture. Sorry, but yes. Harping on the dangers of smoking is not a cliche, especially when you consider that nearly 30 percent of all white-collar workers still smoke. The facts:[8]

- The American Heart Association asserts that approximately 350,000 smokers will die unnecessary deaths this year.†
- Smoking accounts for more than 30 percent of all cancer deaths.‡

---

*Chicago Heart Association, *Salt, Sodium and Blood Pressure* (Dallas: American Heart Association, 1979) p. 2.

†American Heart Association, "Cigarette Smoking and Cardiovascular Disease," *Circulation* (December 1984), p. 1114A.

‡American Cancer Society, *Cancer Facts & Figures–1990* (Atlanta: American Cancer Society, 1990), p. 18.

- Those who smoke two or more packs of cigarettes a day have lung cancer rates 15 to 25 times greater than nonsmokers.*
- At least one out of every six deaths is the result of smoking.†

When people think of the negative or dark side of smoking, they usually think of lung cancer. Yet smoking contributes to many other forms of cancer, emphysema, chronic bronchitis, and heart disease.

Smoking increases your probability of having a heart attack by almost 200 percent. (Heart attacks are responsible for most deaths that come as a direct result of smoking.) Smokers, incidentally, have about 70 percent more heart attacks than nonsmokers.

"Smoking is still considered by most of us to be the number one public health problem in that it causes more preventable deaths and preventable disease than any single controllable force in our environment," says Dr. Eugene Fowinkle, vice chairman of Preventive Medicine at Vanderbilt University Medical School.[9]

Terence Collins, MD, a specialist in preventive medicine at the University of Kentucky, believes that the single best way to improve health is to stop smoking. "Smoking has an impact on multiple risk factors for multiple organ systems," says Dr. Collins. "When you stop smoking, not only are you decreasing the risk factor of cancer, but the mortality decrease that results from smoking cessation as far as the cardiovascular system is concerned is profound."[10]

Good news: Health benefits can begin shortly after you stop smoking. Usually it isn't too late to realize these benefits—provided the body hasn't been significantly damaged. Your risk of getting cancer, heart disease, or emphysema may also decline. It's possible for you to have the same risk factor as someone who never smoked within 10 years of quitting.

You can quit. Do it cold turkey. Or do it gradually. Just do it.

Don't get discouraged if you start back up again. Keep trying to quit until you are successful.

---

*Ibid.
†Ibid.

Hypnosis, special courses, and other activities may also help you to quit smoking. For more information about quitting, call your local chapter of the American Cancer Association.

CONTROL CAFFEINE CONSUMPTION

Drinking coffee is a ritual at just about any office: Ah, the pleasant aroma coffee has when you first come to work in the morning. Later in the day, the smell of coffee seems considerably less pleasant. And by quitting time, its stench is practically rancid.

While most of us drink two to five cups of coffee each day, some people practically addict themselves to food and beverages that are loaded with caffeine. These people often drink 6 to 12 cups of coffee (not the decaffeinated variety) just to get through the workday.

Does caffeine *damage* the cardiovascular system? The results of different studies have not been conclusive. Some studies say yes. Other studies say no.

Since caffeine is a stimulant, it nonetheless stimulates the nervous system. As a result, it may help to constrict blood vessels, raise blood pressure, alter breathing patterns, and influence reactions to stress.

Moreover, caffeine has been linked with headaches, indigestion, insomnia, a higher risk for cancer of the pancreas, and other ailments. Some people also feel nervous after drinking beverages that contain a lot of caffeine.

Until more is known about the side effects of caffeine, view it with suspicion. If caffeine makes you feel nervous, by all means cut down on your consumption of food and beverages such as tea, iced tea, cola drinks, and chocolate that contain it.

DON'T USE ALCOHOL TO COPE WITH STRESS

I won't get on a soapbox and preach what a disaster you'll be on the job if you drink excessive quantities of alcohol to deal with stress. While alcohol abuse can be devastating to home life, many problem drinkers do their jobs well. Most of these people would never come to the office drunk or allow their drinking to interfere with job performance. (But don't drink and drive!)

Although most problem drinkers don't end up homeless or in the gutter, they often jeopardize their health. Years of hard drinking can cause blood pressure to elevate and may make the heart become weak and inefficient. The body then becomes vulnerable to heart disease, cancer, obesity, and many other ailments.

Every day, people who could have been helped by Alcoholics Anonymous or employee assistance programs end up D.O.A. at hospitals because of heart attacks and strokes. You don't have to end up like them.

Try to use the techniques contained in the previous chapter to cope with stress. And don't hesitate to get professional help. You may need more than stress reduction techniques to cope with family or career problems.

HYPERTENSION: BEWARE OF THE SILENT KILLER

While heredity plays a role, it isn't known for sure what causes primary hypertension (commonly called *high blood pressure*) in most people.* Some research indicates that the walls of the arteries constrict when someone has a physical response to stress. This constriction causes the force by which blood flows inside the arteries to rise to higher than normal levels.

If the body operates properly, blood pressure should return to a normal level after a perceived danger has passed. Yet after years of reacting to and recovering from stress, the body may begin to have difficulty returning blood pressure to a normal level. When temporary fluctuations in blood pressure become permanent fluctuations, hypertension occurs.

Although hypertension is not fatal, it nevertheless plays a destructive role in many illnesses that are deadly. Any person who

*American Heart Association, *High Blood Pressure in Teenagers* (Dallas: American Heart Association, 1982), p. 4.

doesn't treat high blood pressure may end up the victim of a heart attack, stroke, or other illness. Hypertension may cause the heart to pump harder, enlarge, weaken, and become less efficient. Since people with hypertension have a reduction in artery capacity, their risk for stroke is increased.

It is estimated that more than one out of every five adults in the United States has high blood pressure (*The Merck Manual*, 1987, p. 392). Hypertension is especially dangerous because more than half the people who have it don't even know that they have it. Usually hypertension doesn't cause pain or exhibit many symptoms that are outwardly visible. Since hypertension damages the body without visible symptoms, many people end up in a hospital intensive care unit before they even know that they have it.

Your blood pressure is commonly measured by two numbers. The systolic (top) number over the diastolic (bottom) number. The National Heart, Lung and Blood Institute has set the following guidelines for blood pressure.*

Systolic = Pressure in arteries when the heart beats

Diastolic = Pressure in arteries when the heart relaxes

General Reference Chart for Adults 18 Years or Older

If Your Reading Is: **You Are Classified:**

Systolic (When Diastolic Blood Pressure is less than 90)
< 140	Normal BP
140—159	Borderline isolated systolic hyertension
> 160	Isolated systolic hypertension

Diastolic Blood Pressure (mm Hg)
< 85	Normal BP
85—89	High Normal BP
90—104	Mild Hypertension
> 115	Severe Hypertension

---

*National High Blood Pressure Educational Treatment Program, *The 1988 Report on the Joint National Committee on Detection Evaluation and Treatment* (Bethesda, MD: National Heart, Lung and Blood Institute 1988) p. 3.

Typically, normal blood pressure ranges from 120–130 for systolic pressure and 70–90 for diastolic pressure. When your systolic blood pressure exceeds 140 and your diastolic number exceeds 90, you need to monitor your blood pressure by taking regular readings. When you consistently have high blood pressure readings of 150/90 or more, you need to seek medical treatment.

It is usually very easy to treat high blood pressure with a variety of special medications. Generally these medications are considered to be lifesaving because they work to lower blood pressure before it causes damage to the body. Although medical treatment is usually required to treat high blood pressure, many people can lower their blood pressure by eating sensibly and by getting regular exercise.

It is always a good idea to have your blood pressure checked regularly. Physicians, clinics, and community centers usually offer to read your blood pressure at no charge or for a nominal fee. You can also read your own blood pressure if you buy an inexpensive blood pressure machine.

GET ENOUGH SLEEP

Many people don't get enough sleep. Think of sleep as recharging and repairing your body in much the same way a tune-up and a grease and lube job keeps a Buick Regal in top condition for another 3,000 miles.

"While people have different patterns of sleep, it's usually advisable to get at least six to eight hours of sleep each night," says Dr. Collins.[11] This helps your body to be physically and mentally ready to tackle the challenges of the next day.

Don't shortchange your body by trying to make do with less sleep. Some people who don't get enough sleep try to get by at work with extra doses of caffeine. However, if you don't get enough sleep, in the long run you risk damaging your heart, getting high blood pressure, and becoming more susceptible to illness.

You must project an image to others that shows you have the vim and vigor to do your job well. Think about it. If you have to get your wisdom teeth pulled, you would probably pick a dentist who was alert and well rested, not one who was listless and hungover.

The message here should be that others may be reluctant to use you in a professional capacity when you act tired.

EXERCISE

In addition to reducing the feelings of anxiety, tiredness, and depression that were described in the previous chapter, an exercise program helps to tone your muscles, burn up calories, and control appetite. More important, if you exercise carefully, you can create a more efficient heart and circulatory system.

According to the American Heart Association, it's a good idea to exercise for 20 to 30 minutes at least three times each week.* When you work out, they recommend exercises that raise your heart and breathing rates. Aerobic exercises should be done in moderation when you make them a part of your exercise program.[12]

Here are some vigorous activities that can condition your heart and lungs, provided you exercise three times a week for more than 20 minutes†:

- Cross-county skiing.
- Hiking.
- Ice hockey.
- Jogging.
- Jumping rope.
- Rowing.

Here are some forms of exercise that can condition your heart

---

*American Heart Association, *Exercise and Your Heart* (Dallas: American Heart Association, 1989), p. 15.
†Ibid., pp. 18–19.

and lungs provided you do them briskly three times a week for at least 30 minutes.

- Running in place.
- Stationary cycling.
- Bicycling.
- Downhill skiing.
- Basketball.
- Calisthenics.
- Field hockey.
- Racquetball.
- Soccer.
- Squash.
- Swimming.
- Tennis (singles).
- Walking.

There are two fundamental rules that should be a part of any se-

That doughnut sure looks good!

rious exercise program. First, get a medical checkup before you start an exercise program. A physician can give you valuable advice about both the types and intensity of exercise that would be beneficial to you. Second, learn how to monitor your heartbeat to guard against physical overexertion and sports-related injuries.

Dr. Fowinkle says, "I think, particularly after a person gets out of their very early adolescence and young adult years, that before one undertakes a major exercise program after having not exercised frequently in the recent past, there should be a medical evaluation before undertaking an exercise program.

"After that, I think the key is to progress slowly. There is a tendency of most of us to jump in like sheriffs and take off down the road and think that we can convert immediately to Olympic-type athletes. That just isn't true. If we take weeks, months, or years to build a very strong exercise program gradually, I think the likelihood of danger is minimal," says Dr. Fowinkle.[13]

Request a physical examination before you start an exercise program even if one isn't covered by your health insurance. Since many serious heart abnormalities often do not reveal their presence in less strenuous EKG tests, Dr. Kottke of the Mayo Clinic advises that you ask your physician to give you a stress electrocardiogram if you're over 40 or have other risk factors for heart disease.

"The difference between a resting cardiogram and a stress test is like the difference between looking at a used car on the lot and driving it. It may look great, but the motor might not even start." As a result, Dr. Kottke believes that the heart needs to be revved up during a stress test to see if it runs right.[14]

Once you have had a medical evaluation, you need to learn how to check your heartbeat periodically during and immediately after exercise to see if you are putting too much strain on your heart. This can be done by taking your pulse.

Your maximum heartbeat is the fastest that your heart can beat (100 percent of capacity). According to the American Heart Association, people who start new exercise programs should try to keep their heart rate close to 60 percent of its maximum capacity during the first few months. Once they get into better condition, they can gradually build up to the 75 percent level.* This 60–75 percent range is commonly called your target zone. At the end of six months, the association says that you can exercise up to 85 percent of your maximum capacity. However, this isn't necessary because you can stay in good condition by working out in the 60 to 75 percent level.†

The American Heart Association says to take your pulse immediately after you stop exercising. Here's how you can check if you're within your target heart rate zone:

Age	60–75% Target Zone	Average Maximum Heart Rates at 100 Percent
20	120–150	200
25	117–146	195
30	114–142	190
35	111–138	185
40	108–135	180
45	105–131	175
50	102–127	170
55	99–123	165
60	96–120	160
65	93–116	155
70	90–113	150

Source: American Heart Association, *Exercise and Your Heart*, pp. 18–19.

1. After you stop exercising, quickly place the tips of your first two fingers lightly over one of the blood vessels on your neck (carotid arteries). These vessels are located to the left or right of your Adam's apple. Another convenient pulse spot is the inside of your wrist just below the base of your thumb.
2. Counting your pulse for 10 seconds and multiplying by six to get your heart rate per minute count.

---

*American Heart Association, *Exercise and Your Heart* (Dallas: American Heart Association, 1989), p. 18–19.
†Ibid.

TIP

Make Exercise Fun

"People need to make their exercise programs enjoyable, exhilarating, and not painful," says Dr. James Marx of the Centers for Disease Control. "Exercise should not be an incredible tedium or chore." So don't jump into a program too quickly. "You might get an injury or stop the program too soon."[15]

---

3. Once you're exercising within your target, you should check your pulse at least once each week during the first three months and periodically thereafter.

If your pulse is below your target zone, exercise a little harder the next time. If you're above your target zone, exercise a little easier. And if it falls within your target zone, you are doing fine. (Note: Medicine for high blood pressure can affect your heart rate. If you use such medication ask your physician for advice about your target rate.)

To get more information about an exercise program, read any of the following aerobic exercise books written by Kenneth H. Cooper, MD:

- *The Aerobics Program for Total Well-being* (Bantam Books)
- *The Aerobics Way* (Bantam Books)
- *The New Aerobics for Women* (Bantam Books)
- *Running Without Fear* (Bantam Books)

WEAR SAFETY BELTS

I realize that wearing safety belts in a motor vehicle has nothing to do with the level of cholesterol in your blood and other health problems. Yet it is no secret that the leading cause of death for people ages 1 to 38 in the United States is motor vehicle crashes.[16]

Each year, more than 1.7 million people are injured and 45,000

TIP

Ideal body weight for women is roughly 105 pounds plus 5 pounds for every inch of height over 5 feet. For men, ideal body weight is roughly 106 pounds plus 6 pounds for every inch of height over 5 feet. If you're a 5′ 8″ male, you should weigh about 154 pounds (106 + 8 × 6 = 154).

Medical Warning
Seek proper medical advice from your physician prior to undertaking any physical exercise or procedure, or undertaking any health care recommendation.

---

people die in motor vehicle related crashes.[17] Most new cases of paraplegia are the result of injuries to the spinal cord sustained in vehicle accidents. And head injuries received in automobile accidents often bring on epilepsy.

"About 50 percent of all deaths and injuries sustained in motor vehicle related accidents could have been avoided if safety belts had been worn," says Timothy P. Kennedy, coordinator of the National Safety Council's occupant protection program. In spite of those statistics, "only 49 percent of Americans wear safety belts when they travel in a motor vehicle."[18]

You might think that you don't need to wear safety belts when you travel short distances. But the National Safety Council believes that about 80 percent of all automobile crashes occur at speeds of less than 40 miles per hour. And those crashes usually occur within 25 miles of the victim's home. So if you're not wearing safety belts, even at a slow speed such as 30 miles per hour, a sudden stop can force you to slam into the windshield or dashboard—at a speed of 30 miles per hour.[19]

Many people don't wear safety belts because they fear being trapped in a fire or underwater. Yet the National Safety Council stresses that fire and submersion rarely play a significant role in injury-producing collisions.[20]

Survival rates are 25 times greater for someone who wears a safety belt than for someone who is thrown out of a vehicle in a crash. And if you wear safety belts, you're more likely to stay conscious and escape from a car that's on fire or under water.[21]

When my sister Fawn and I were kids, Dad used to insist we wear safety belts. So we got in the habit of buckling up. (We had to if we wanted Dad to drive us to the mall.)

Good thing. Years later, when I was a student at Florida State University, a truck pulled out in front of my Chevy. Click! Then—Crash! In a split second, those safety belts pulled into action. To make a long story short, my car suffered a lot of damage, but I didn't. Thanks, Dad!

AT A GLANCE

Red alert: You might not be adopting a healthy lifestyle fast enough. Failure to do so may result in future declines in your health and productivity.

While our health care system has made great progress in educating people about preventive medicine, it's still adapted to treating the seriously ill. Too many physicians don't emphasize preventive medicine. And thousands of others don't incorporate risk factor appraisal in their practices.

Think how many people with clogged arteries could have avoided heart bypass surgery if they had only exercised, controlled stress, and ate sensibly. That's just one example, but it shows the need to take responsibility for your health.

Take the initiative—incorporate a program of wellness into your life. Here's a recap of what it takes to be a winner in the wellness department.

- Part 1: Try to prevent a physical reaction to stress by monitoring and controlling your thoughts.
- Part 2: When you have a physical reaction to stress, try to bring about relaxation by using meditation, exercise, or relaxation tapes.

- Part 3: Use these eight wellness rules to enhance your health:

  1. Don't let your arteries look like jelly doughnuts.
  2. Stop smoking.
  3. Control caffeine consumption.
  4. Don't use alcohol to cope with stress.
  5. Hypertension: beware of the silent killer.
  6. Get enough sleep.
  7. Exercise.
  8. Wear safety belts.

CHAPTER 10   AUTHOR INTERVIEWS

1. Cliff Lothery, August 16, 1988.
2. David Emorling, June 1, 1990.
3. Ibid.
4. Charles Arnold, May 25, 1990.
5. Thomas Kottke, June 1, 1990.
6. Ibid.
7. James Marx, October 14, 1988.
8. National Center for Health Statistics, Kathy Santini, May 25, 1990.
9. Eugene Fowinkle, August 19, 1988.
10. Terence Collins, June 1, 1990.
11. Collins, December 11, 1990.
12. Fowinkle, August 19, 1988.
13. Ibid.
14. Kottke, June 1, 1990.
15. Marx, October 14, 1988.
16. Timothy P. Kennedy, December 12, 1990.
17. Ibid.
18. Ibid.
19. Ibid.
20. Ibid.
21. Ibid.

Chapter Eleven

Gotta Make a Buck Somehow

The results are in.

First, what you should know about the informal surveys: They were mailed to selected Jaycees' chapters in the U.S.*

You might be saying, "Why people who were Jaycees?" Well, I wanted a natural database of white-collar men and *women*. That's right, women—more than 46 percent of people who responded to the survey were women. And I wanted a group that included young business people, recent college graduates, and middle managers. (Note: the survey responses reflect individual opinions and situations, not the Jaycees Organization.)

Age of Respondents

Age	Percent of Total Respondents
21–25	21%
26–30	39
31–35	28
36–39	9
40–49	3

*The survey was created, sponsored, tabulated, and evaluated by Jim G. Germer.

And I wanted a well-educated population. More than 80 percent had at least some college. More specifically, 42 percent had college degrees, and another 15 percent had postgraduate degrees.

Highest Level of Education of People Surveyed

Highest Education Level	Percent of Total Respondents
High school	16%
Some college	25
College	42
Postgraduate	15
Other	2

And what kind of jobs did they have? Most respondents were managers, professionals, or worked in sales or business and finance. But a significant percentage worked in technical and secretarial positions.

Each Jaycees' president passed out the questionnaires at a general membership meeting, then collected them and returned them to me for tabulation. Signing names was optional.

This informal survey yields some interesting statistics on what these people say it's like for them to be white-collar workers these days. Let's take a look at what the 938 respondents had to say.

LOVE AT WORK: IS IT WORTH THE RISK?

Psychologists and management professors often say work is a good place to meet a spouse. You spend a lot of time at work. You get to observe the other person. And if you're a single parent, you might not get many opportunities to meet people outside of work.

Yes, I know it's next to impossible to find Mr. Right or Miss Perfect in a bar. And that nice-looking co-worker looks a lot better than a lounge lizard.

Still, nearly 40 percent of my survey felt dating a boss or co-worker is a mistake. And another 33 percent believe that you should avoid dating a boss or co-worker, or at least date someone in another department. Only 6 percent believe that dating at work doesn't create any problems for an employee. So a majority of respondents, 73 percent, view dating bosses and co-workers negatively. You have to wonder, ''Are these people talking from experience?'' I wouldn't be surprised.

When I conducted interviews personally, many managers said they prefer that their employees not date co-workers. Many even said they try to subtly break up such relationships because they create problems within the department such as favoritism, sexual harassment suits, rumors, missed promotions, or having to work next to someone who broke your heart.

But love and hormones often interfere with good judgment. So the question comes up once *again*, ''Should you or shouldn't you?''

The safe strategy is avoid it if career advancement is your number one priority. No involvement, no hassle.

But if love is your number one priority, you might start a relationship. If it works out, I hope you have a great married life. But if it doesn't, update your resume.

HEY, PEOPLE ARE GETTING FIRED

Now, this was interesting. One out of every five people surveyed said they had been fired or quit a job before they would have been fired. Remember, these are young people; the median age group was 26–30. And that's not even counting people who lose jobs in layoffs.

Firings are a quick fix. Good managers work at salvaging employees. I think this will be one of the big challenges for managers in the 1990s.

Firings and layoffs are one career obstacle you should be on the lookout for; read Chapter 8 if your job is at risk.

WHY DO YOU THINK PEOPLE GET FIRED?

Speaking of getting fired, respondents were asked, "Why do you think people get fired?"

You know the old stigma, "Anyone who gets fired is an incompetent loser who couldn't do his or her job." (Code name, poor performance) Well, contrary to that managerial belief, the number one answer to why people were fired was employees and employers who have different goals and expectations. Let's take a closer look at how most people answered:

Different Expectations: 28 Percent.   Could it be the clash between New Breed upbringings and the Old Breed? Or could it be New Breed managers who are impatient for results from their own New Breed employees?

Poor Attitude: 22 Percent.   Poor attitude got a lot of votes, too. Sometimes a bad attitude gets a bad reputation. Why? To put it simply, something always causes a bad attitude.

For example, a manager promises a promotion. Then she forgets the promise and promotes someone else. The employee is hurt and does not discuss it with his manager. Disappointment leads to less productivity and a change in disposition, forcing the manager to fire the now "bad" employee.

Personality Conflicts: 15 Percent.   Problems with people were another big winner. We addressed these earlier in Chapter 8. Still, I would like to say, "If you are unhappy in a negative organization where you feel repressed or depressed, *change jobs!*"

Don't stay where the chemistry is wrong! Go someplace where you don't feel anxious and where you're appreciated.

If you are responsible for some of the conflicts, get human relations training. Work at getting along better with co-workers and superiors.

Poor Performance: 25 percent. This is the one that management textbooks focus on. But we're talking people here, not computers or other depreciable assets.

Companies, try to save your poor performers. You hire someone. You train that person. Then if someone is not immediately productive, you might fire that person. "You're not living up to your potential," or "We expected more out of you," you say.

Maybe. But what ends up happening is employees take the training and experience to their next job. Often they become superstars. You're out a sizable investment. And their new employer saves a fortune in training costs on the model you just broke in.

CHANGING JOBS: CAREER HOPPING IS NOT CAREER PATHING

Job changing is a way of life for a New Breeder. Sometimes it works and sometimes it doesn't. If you do it compulsively, you won't be able to achieve many of your goals. If you jump to a better opportunity, fine. But sooner or later, you should commit—you'll need a pension.

Respondents have changed jobs a lot. More than 50 percent of respondents said they had three or more jobs since age 21. More than 21 percent of respondents said they had four to six jobs. And another 6 percent said they had more than seven jobs.

The method is, "Keep changing jobs until one clicks." In America, there is a dichotomy between companies that say, "Where are all the good people?" and "Where are the truly good managers?" and the glut of New Breeders waiting for someone to give them a chance.

Job changing can be a healthy thing if you continue to make big strides up the career ladder. But if you don't earn as much money or you're not as high up the ladder, either you're changing jobs too much or you need an individual advancement program.

HEY, PAL, YOU'RE NOT MAKING IT

Since graduation, are you at the point in your career that you thought you would be?

1. No, I don't earn as much money and I'm not as high up the company ladder as I thought I would be (34 percent).
2. I'm at roughly the same place that I thought I would be (33 percent).
3. My career is progressing nicely. I'm higher up the ladder than I thought I would be (28 percent).

Since graduation, are you at the point in your career that you thought you would be? The number one answer was *no*! More than 34 percent said they don't earn as much money and aren't as high up the ladder as they thought they would be. Almost 33 percent said they were roughly at the same place. And another lucky 28 percent had progressed further than expected. (Five percent declined to answer.)

Who would have thought that more than 34 percent of the people surveyed said they thought they would have gone a lot further since graduation? All that education, and they're still not high up the career ladder or earning big money.

This was the most provocative statistic.

Here are some *possible* reasons why these people are having problems finding money and success:

The Pack Isn't Moving Fast Enough.   A traffic jam of bright baby boomers may keep your career in a holding pattern. When it comes to money and opportunity, you had better take charge of your own career.

Maturity.   Your college expectations are out of whack with the real world. You think you're going to start with a snazzy foreign car and $35,000 a year, but find you have to settle for a Ford and $19,500.

Do Dreams Die First?   Too many chiefs and not enough indians does not a partnership make. Large international professional

firms hire eager college graduates with the lure of future partner-
ships. "Yes, you can make partner in 10 years, and when you do—
you'll earn six figures," the recruiter says. But what the recruiter
doesn't say is how many people *actually* make partner. If the recruiter did, most people wouldn't sign on.

WHY SURVEYED EMPLOYEES LEFT THEIR LAST JOB

Let's take a look at why these people left their last job. Was it because
management lacked integrity? Was it because people weren't progressing in their firms? Was it problems with bosses and co-workers?
Was it a volatile economy? No. No. No. And no. The number one
answer was they wanted a job with more *money* and *opportunity*.

Now what does this say about the money and opportunity at
their last job?

Why They Left Their Last Job

Percent of Total Respondents	Reason for Leaving
8%	Lack of management integrity
9	Not happy with rate progressing at company
4	Problems getting along with boss or co-workers
8	Victim of economy
47	Wanted a job with more money and opportunity
24	Other reasons

HOW EMPLOYEES LIKE THEIR EMPLOYERS

Respondents seem to like the companies they work for. More than
two out of three rated their employers good or excellent. And another 24 percent rated their companies average. Only 6 percent of
respondents rated their employers poor or failing.

So the paradox is: Why do people keep changing jobs if they like the companies they work for?

Maybe the pack isn't moving fast enough: New Breeders don't want to *grow* into middle- and top-management jobs—they want those jobs now! (That's if the opportunities exist. Waiting for a slot is one thing; but waiting for a slot that doesn't exist is another.)

Or maybe their companies are tight with a buck? Money talks or New Breeders walk.

Nabbing a corner office is going to be tougher than ever in the '90s. Companies are trimming their middle- and upper-management ranks. So hedge your bets for money and success with an individual advancement program. Make use of *How to Make Your Boss Work for You.*

AT A GLANCE

Many people surveyed said:

- They're having trouble turning diplomas into money and success.
- Dating a boss or co-worker is a mistake.
- They like the companies they work for.
- They have had many jobs since graduation.
- They change jobs to get more *money* and *opportunity*.
- They've been fired.
- Employees and employers with different goals and expectations are responsible for most firings.

A Final Word

If you're in over your head, I hope this book gets you out of the quicksand. And if you already have a corner office, I wish you even more success. May this book help you nab a plush executive suite with a wet bar, private bathroom, executive secretary, 401K plan, stock options, company car. . . .

Recommended Reading

CAREER DEVELOPMENT

Bolles, Richard. *What Color Is Your Parachute?* Berkeley: Ten Speed Press, 1984.

DuBrin Andrew. *Winning Office Politics: Durbin's New Guide for the 90's.* Englewood Cliffs, N.J.: Prentice Hall, 1990.

Gould, Richard. *Sacked! Why Good People Get Fired and How to Avoid It.* New York: John Wiley & Sons, 1986.

Half, Robert. *Robert Half on Hiring.* New York: Crown Publishers, 1985.

Higginson, Margaret, and Thomas L. Quick. *The Ambitious Woman's Guide to a Successful Career.* New York: AMACOM, 1980.

Imundo, Louis V. *The Effective Supervisor's Handbook.* New York: AMACOM, 1980.

Kennedy, Marilyn Moats. *Office Politics: Seizing Power, Wielding Clout.* New York: Warner Books, 1987.

Kiechel, Walter. *Office Hours: A Guide to the Managerial Life.* Boston: Little, Brown, 1988.

Leibowitz, Zandy B. et al., *Designing Career Development Systems.* San Francisco: Jossey-Bass, 1986.

Maccoby, Michael. *Why Work: Leading the New Generation.* New York: Touchtone, 1988.

Peskin, Dean. *Sacked! What to Do When You Lose Your Job.* New York: AMACOM, 1979.

Roesch, Roberta. *You Can Make It without a College Degree.* Englewood Cliffs, N.J.: Prentice Hall, 1986.

Souerwine, Andrew. *Career Strategies.* New York: AMACOM, 1980.

Waitley, Dennis, and Reni L. Witt. *The Joy of Working.* New York: Ballantine Books, 1986.

HUMAN RELATIONS AND COMMUNICATIONS TRAINING

Carnegie, Dale. *How to Win Friends and Influence People.* New York: Simon & Schuster, 1981.

Chapman, Elwood N. *Your Attitude Is Showing.* Chicago: Science Research Associates, 1987.

Maltz, Maxwell. *Magic Power of Self-Image Psychology.* Englewood Cliffs, N.J.: Prentice Hall, 1989.

STRESS MANAGEMENT

Benson, Herbert, and Miriam Z. Klipper. *The Relaxation Response.* New York: Avon Books, 1976.

Eliot, Robert S., and Dennis L. Breo. *Is It Worth Dying For?* New York: Bantam Books, 1989.

Goldberg, Philip. *Executive Health.* New York: McGraw-Hill, 1979.

Jacobson, Edmund. *Progressive Relaxation.* Chicago: University of Chicago Press, 1974.

Selye, Hans. *Stress without Distress.* New York: New American Library, 1975.

HEALTH AND FITNESS

Cooper, Kenneth H. *Controlling Cholesterol.* New York: Bantam Books, 1988.

Kerson, Toba Schwaber. *Understanding Chronic Illness.* New York: The Free Press, 1985.

Mayo Clinic. *Mayo Clinic Family Health and Medical Guide.* New York: Greenwillow/Morrow, 1990.

Rosenfeld, Isadore. *Symptoms.* New York: Simon & Schuster, 1987.

Scala, James. *The High Blood Pressure Relief Diet*. New York: New American Library, 1989.

MANAGEMENT

Blanchard, Kenneth, and Spencer Johnson. *The One Minute Manager*. New York: Berkley Books, 1987.

Carnevale, Anthony P. et al., *Workplace Basics: The Essential Skills Employers Want*. San Francisco: Jossey-Bass, 1990.

_____ *Workplace Basics Training Manual*, San Francisco: Jossey-Bass, 1990.

Cribbin, James J. *Leadership: Strategies for Organizational Effectiveness*. New York: AMACOM, 1982.

Drucker, Peter F. *The Effective Executive*. New York: Harper & Row, 1985.

_____ *The Frontiers of Management*. New York: E. P. Dutton, 1987.

_____ *Managing in Turbulent Times*. New York: Harper & Row, 1980.

_____ *The Practice of Management*. New York: Harper & Row, 1986.

Hannaway, Jane. *Managers Managing: The Workings of an Administrative System*. New York: Oxford Univ. Press, 1989.

Kanter, Rosabeth Moss. *Men and Women of the Corporation*. New York: Basic Books, 1977.

Kilmann, Ralph H. *Managing Beyond the Quick Fix*. San Francisco: Jossey-Bass, 1989.

Kotter, John P. *A Force For Change: How Leadership Differs from Management*. New York: The Free Press, 1990.

_____ *The Leadership Factor*. New York: The Free Press, 1988.

Levitt, Theodore. *Thinking about Management*. New York: The Free Press, 1990.

Montana, Patrick. *Management*. New York: Baron's, 1987.

Odiorne, George S. *How Managers Make Things Happen*. Englewood Cliffs, N.J.: Prentice Hall, 1987.

_____ *The Human Side of Management*. Lexington, Mass.: Lexington Books, 1987.

Zaleznik, Abraham. *The Managerial Mystique*. New York: Harper & Row, 1989.

Index